**How We Are Our Enemy
– And How to Stop**

ALSO BY JOHN L. HODGE

BOOK AND BOOK CHAPTERS:

"Equality: Beyond Dualism and Oppression," Chapter 6 of *Anatomy of Racism* (1990)

"Democracy and Free Speech: A Normative Theory of Society and Government," Chapter 5 of *The First Amendment Reconsidered* (1982)

Cultural Bases of Racism and Group Oppression: An Examination of Traditional "Western" Concepts, Values and Institutional Structures Which Support Racism, Sexism and Elitism (co-author) (1975)

JOURNAL ARTICLE:

"Deadlocked-Jury Mistrials, Lesser Included Offenses, and Double Jeopardy: A Proposal to Strengthen the Manifest Necessity Requirement," *Criminal Justice Journal* (Vol. 9, No. 1) (1986)

How We Are Our Enemy – And How to Stop

OUR UNFINISHED TASK OF
FULFILLING THE VALUES OF DEMOCRACY

John L. Hodge
J.D., Ph.D.

John L. Hodge
Publisher

Published in the U.S.A,
by
John L. Hodge, Publisher
P. O. Box 301377
Jamaica Plain, Massachusetts 02130
U.S.A.
JLHPublisher@gmail.com
Your comments are appreciated.
Order books from retailers.

**For more information,
go to the website at
http://johnlhodge.com**

ISBN: 978-0-9831790-0-9

Print on demand services provided by Lightning Source, Inc.

**Printed copies available through
local and online bookstores.** Check for
ebook availability.

CONTENTS

The so-called "golden rule," properly understood, is the ethical source of democratic values.

The growth of democracy is up to us.

ACKNOWLEDGMENTS

Although the final text is fully my responsibility, I thank Anna Sears, James Reed, and my spouse, Diane Franklin, for their valuable editorial assistance. I also thank Diane and my son, Jascha Franklin-Hodge, for their thoughtful discussions of politics and other matters that helped me think through some of the ideas in this book.

INTRODUCTION

Democratic values are the ethical foundation of democracy. When we affirm these values, we further the progress toward fuller democracy. When we lose sight of them, we allow democracy to deteriorate, and then we become its enemy.

Our adherence to these values typically weakens in times of stress. For example, a widespread abandonment of these values occurred during the presidency of George W. Bush following the attacks on the World Trade Center and the Pentagon that occurred on September 11, 2001. Under stress and fear, the United States and many other "democratic" nations abandoned democratic values in favor of an ever-present anti-democratic mentality that has survived from the anti-democratic past of humankind. Such abandonment will be continued or repeated if we do not get a better grip on what democratic values truly mean—for it was the American public and the supporting publics of other nations who abandoned these values, not just the President.

Thus, we are sadly mistaken when we think the security of democracy depends primarily on defeating an external enemy.

This does not mean that we should fail to protect ourselves from external attack, but it does mean that successfully protecting ourselves still leaves us vulnerable to the decay or abandonment of the values that underlie the kind of society we are trying to protect. Putting primary focus on an external enemy diverts our attention from the main task at hand.

The responsibility for preventing regression to the anti-democratic ways of the past and for advancing democratic values rests on the shoulders of every one of us. Advancing democratic values requires, among other things, realizing our personal responsibility and seeing how these values affect all facets of our lives. Democracy is not just a political structure. Our values, our personal beliefs and the social and political policies we support are intertwined.

We see this intertwining of personal beliefs and political policies on many fronts. Personal beliefs about individual responsibility affect whether we support welfare benefits, social security or universal health care. Personal beliefs about the role of women affect the extent to which we support equal rights for women. Personal beliefs about abortion affect whether we support an individual woman's right to choose to have one. Personal beliefs about homosexuality affect whether we support the rights of gays to marry. These are just a few examples where personal beliefs are also beliefs about what should be national policies.

However, the national policies that would flow from our personal beliefs may conflict with another belief—the belief in democracy. If we keep our personal beliefs compartmentalized and separate from the values underlying democracy, we avoid seeing the conflict. But the conflict is often there. Democracy falters when these conflicts are not acknowledged and resolved.

Such conflicts are not new. Typically and historically there has been a disconnection between widespread personal beliefs and the values of democracy. The signers of the Declaration of Independence in 1776 declared in the same document the fundamental democratic value that "all men are created equal" and that Native Americans are "merciless Indian savages." They could not see an obvious inconsistency that, fortunately, we can see today. They also could not see the obvious inconsistency between democracy and slavery. Those who established the U.S. Constitution, believing that they were establishing the legal foundation for a democracy, ratified a document that acknowledged slavery and that permitted the denial of women's right to vote. Their personal beliefs about the role and status of women, slaves and Native Americans were disconnected from their voicing the values underlying democracy. By not making the connection, they could not see the inconsistencies between their personal beliefs and the values of democracy. This disconnection allowed them to think falsely that democracy and the society they lived in were essentially synonymous. They were quite wrong. How could this have happened?

And is it different today? How is it that today, for example, in the United States we can so often see little or no conflict between the society we live in and the values of democracy? How can we claim to live in a democracy and at the same time see that, even when a member of a minority group has become President of the United States, there nonetheless remains a significant underrepresentation of women minorities at the highest levels of governments and in corporate boardrooms, and a dramatic over-representation of minorities among those who are impoverished or imprisoned? How is it that, in our democracy, the proposed Equal Rights Amendment, which would put the guarantee of equal rights for women into the U.S. Constitution, still has not been ratified by enough states to make it law? How is it that, in our democracy, in most states, we do not give the same recognition to families consisting of same-gender couples and their children as we give to families consisting of opposite-gender couples and their children? How is it that, in our democracy, we have for so long accepted that health care can be denied to those who cannot afford to pay for it, while the attempt to provide health care for all meets with virulent opposition? And how is it that, in our democracy, our government can initiate a devastating war against another country, initially with the full support of a majority of the public?

Believing that we do live in accordance with our professed values blinds us to seeing when we do not. Just as the Founders were blind to the severe flaws in the society they thought was a democracy, so are we. The flaws are different, but they are very serious flaws nonetheless. They are flaws that not only threaten the progress made to date toward greater democracy but also threaten to reverse our direction and cause a retreat from democracy and a return to the anti-democratic practices of the past.

We are constantly encouraged to blind ourselves to these flaws by politicians asserting that the United States is the greatest country on earth and that God blesses America, as though God somehow prefers America to elsewhere in the world. Any political candidate who says otherwise is subject to ridicule and doomed to defeat in an election. But thinking this way confuses the existing flawed society with the goal to be achieved. This way of thinking supports a complacency that not only is the greatest enemy to further progress toward building a fully democratic society but also is the congenial companion to retreat from democratic values, for it allows us to believe falsely that what we do is what ought to be done.

Nowhere have the values of democracy been fully realized. Societies now called "democracies" are not full democracies but, at best, societies in the midst of a long historical development that has yet to be completed. The United States is no exception.

Nonetheless, we should not overlook the enormous progress that has been made by societies that have emerged from the vast undemocratic past of humankind, a "past" that is still present in much of the world. These societies we call "democracies," including our own, generally have a sufficiently sound legal and social framework that is open to change and allows for further realization of democratic values. Such change occurred, for example, in the United States when slavery that existed legally at the time of the American revolution was abolished through an amendment to the U.S. Constitution in 1865. It occurred when women were guaranteed the right to vote through an amendment to the U.S. Constitution in 1920. It occurred in 2008 when the people of the United States elected as President a person who, prior to the Civil Rights Act of 1964, could have been legally denied a job, barred from a restroom, or arrested for drinking at the nearest water fountain solely because of the color of his skin. These changes took quite a while to occur, but occur they did.

But this same openness to change that holds the hope of the future also allows existing democracies to turn backwards and reject the very values upon which they are based. This is the ever-present danger lurking within any society that has adopted a democratic political structure. The very openness necessary for further progress allows for anti-democratic views and ideologies to grow and become dominant. These anti-democratic ways of thinking are typically homegrown and emanate not only from isolated enclaves of ordinary people but also from nationally recognized intellectual and political leaders.

These anti-democratic ways of thinking cannot be forcibly suppressed without turning against the values of democracy. These values require, among other things, freedom of expression and freedom to associate with others. The only thing that prevents our retrogression is our own constant effort to help democracy grow. This effort requires that we keep democratic values constantly present in our consciousnesses, openly express them, and work incessantly to fulfill them.

But increasingly in recent years this is not what we have done. We have become complacent and falsely satisfied with our presumed greatness, thus blinding ourselves to the depth of our failures. In this way we have become the enemies of the democratic values we profess, for we honor these values in words only, but defeat them with a complacency that allows forces that oppose these values to grow and thrive. As these forces grow and thrive, they can result in the election of those who share these anti-democratic views and ideologies and support initiatives and policies that have no place in a truly democratic society.

Allowing anti-democratic thinking to ascend is what happened when, with the support of the vast majority of the U.S. Congress and the American public, the United States invaded Iraq in 2003. It was not a hasty, ill-planned, thoughtless venture like the 2001 invasion of Afghanistan, but one that was thoroughly premeditated and examined publicly in advance. This invasion, and especially the widespread mentality behind it, was one of the biggest setbacks for democracy since the end of slavery.

By invading Iraq, the United States began a war supposedly to impose democracy where it did not exist. But, as will become clearer as we examine the meaning of democratic values, the very attempt to impose democracy by military force is destructive of what democracy stands for. Real democracy—that is, democracy based on democratic values—cannot be imposed on others; it can only be imposed by people who want it for themselves, impose it upon themselves, and believe in the values that preserve it. If they do not have democracy, they must create it for themselves, where the energy of their own beliefs enables them to ignore or dispose of tyrants. If they themselves do not have this energy, it cannot be handed to them on a platter from abroad, especially not on a platter filled with the blood and body parts of their own people.

But that is what the United States tried to do with its invasion, at the cost of hundreds of thousands of lives. Iraq now clings to the outward trappings of democracy that may or may not take root and grow, while its internal violence reveals that the ethical foundation of democracy may not be widespread enough for real democracy to survive. The relatives and friends of those who died as a direct or indirect consequence of the invasion were given good reason to doubt that what the invaders called "democracy" is a good thing.

The mentality that made the invasion possible paid little attention to the blood spilled by the Iraqi people. The ignoring and belittling of the extensive Iraqi deaths revealed that the invasion was not actually about spreading democratic values, values that view others as equals. Instead, it was primarily about a global struggle for power and control where the Iraqi people were treated like unequal pawns. This mentality is not only a mentality favoring military aggression, it is also a mentality that supports torture, prolonged imprisonment of suspects without trial, deprivation of privacy, and centralized power concentrated in the hands of a single chief executive—

all of which has happened. This mentality—a mentality derived from ancient but persistent anti-democratic paradigms described in Chapter 2—is still present in the United States, and though it may have subsided somewhat toward the end of the administration of George W. Bush, it still lies just beneath the surface and threatens to reemerge when the conditions are again right for fear to dominate our psyches.

This anti-democratic mentality will remain strong even when hidden, regardless of the outcome of elections, if we do not vigorously reassert the values of democracy. To the extent we adopt that mentality or do not actively counteract it, we ourselves become enemies of democracy.

The energy that creates and sustains democracy is not generated by military strength or economic dominance or spread by invasions but must come from the strength of our values and the determination to put these values into action. Just as this energy is needed to create and sustain democracy, so does a weakening of this energy permit existing democracy to degenerate into increasing submission to centralized authority and enhanced erosion of basic civil liberties. This weakening has already happened in the United States, and it will continue to get worse if we do not vigorously reassert the values of democracy in all facets of our lives.

Advancing democratic values goes well beyond the political arena. These values manifest in the way we live day-to-day, treat others, and interact with our social, political and natural environment. Over many decades, these values have changed the way we personally relate to our spouses, treat our children, and treat others from different ethnic, national, religious or economic backgrounds. The values of democracy link the personal and the political and make them inseparable. They tie together the attitudes we have toward others in our personal lives with the national and international policies we support.

The historical progress of democracy has been slow but steady, in spite of many severe setbacks. It is the values of democracy that generate this progress, and it is the weakening of these values that allow for the setbacks. There is no historical guarantee that the setbacks will not ultimately prevail and assign democracy to a short chapter in human history. That is the danger we face today.

What are these values of democracy? In what ways have we turned against them? How can we consistently affirm them instead? What are the persistent anti-democratic paradigms from the past that still stand in the way? This book provides answers to these questions and shows how democratic values are based on a sound and lasting ethical foundation. With a higher level of understanding of the ethical foundation of democracy, we can resume our historic trek toward greater democracy and not be thwarted and misled by the persistent historical forces that push backwards toward the past.

This historical trek depends on each of us, for building a democratic society depends not on authorities, rulers or elected officials, but on our own efforts and values.

Chapter 1

How We Could Affirm the Values of Democracy—And Often Don't

> *We do not yet fully understand the meaning of equality.*

The principle of human equality is the fundamental value underlying democracy. All other values of democracy arise from this principle. It has profound ramifications, many of which we are still learning. This principle applies not only to political and social policies but also to the way we interact with others and think about them in our daily lives.

The Principle of Equality

The principle of equality was proclaimed as the fundamental democratic value in the Declaration of Independence: "All men are created equal." Abraham Lincoln reaffirmed this central principle in his famous Gettysburg Address: "Four score and seven years ago our fathers brought forth on this continent, a new nation, conceived in Liberty, and dedicated to the proposition that all men are created equal." This principle was again affirmed by President Barack Obama at his inauguration on January 20, 2009: "The time has come to reaffirm our enduring spirit; to choose our better history; to carry forward that precious gift, that noble idea, passed on from generation to generation: the God-given promise that all are equal, all are free, and all deserve a chance to pursue their full measure of happiness."

While the principle of equality was clearly stated in the Declaration of Independence, its full ramifications were not understood. Among other things, there is no indication that the writers of the Declaration of Independence intended to extend full equality to women. Lincoln credited the "fathers" and implicitly ignored the contributions women made. Today we understand that the central principle of democracy must say, "All *people* are created equal."

But, just as the Founders did not see this and other ramifications, there are still many ramifications that we do not see.

What *are* the full ramifications of this principle?

If it means anything, it means that every human life has a worth equal to every other human life. To former president John Quincy Adams, who should be considered among the Founders, this translated into a Constitution based on the "principle of equal rights."[1] The concept of equal rights is implicit in the Declaration's assertion that governments must derive "their just powers from the consent of the governed." The "governed" includes everyone, without special favor to anyone, without exclusion of anyone. In choosing our governmental representatives, everyone is provided the opportunity to participate and be treated equally.

Equal rights apply to everyone regardless of their

circumstances or achievements. Thus, "all people are created equal" cannot mean that we are only created equal at birth but that equality disappears as we grow older, and that we become unequal depending on what we do, what we own, and who we are. If this were true, democracy would not mean one person, one vote, but that some people's votes should count more than others depending on their circumstances or achievements. But today—though not initially—we have come to understand that "all people are created equal" means, among other things, one person, one vote, and proportional representation. This understanding means that "all people are created equal" is not just about what we are at birth, but about what we continue to be throughout our lives. Our equality does not depend on our circumstances or achievements.

The principle of equality also does not mean that everyone must have equal wealth. Worth and wealth are not the same thing. But this does not mean that all disparities of wealth are acceptable. The principle of equality also does not mean that everyone should be reduced to sameness. To think everyone should be alike denies the equal worth of those who are different. Equality and sameness are not the same and are even contradictory. Equality is equality of human worth that is not diminished by our differences.

Democracy as a Work in Progress

Although we may think that we understand it, this short, apparently simple principle has enormous consequences that to this day we still do not fully understand. The writers of this fundamental principle, those considered among America's Founders, clearly did not understand its full meaning. In this respect, in spite of considerable progress, we are not different from them.

For example, the Founders failed to connect this sound principle to their own society and personal behavior. When the Declaration was written in 1776, blacks were enslaved, and some of the Founders owned slaves. Native Americans were being intentionally killed. Women had no right to vote. Married women were the legal property of men. Most people were not thought of as equal. Only property-owning white males were equal enough to vote, people like the Founders themselves. The principle of "one person, one vote" was not fully developed until much later in the mid-twentieth century.[2]

The Founders, in other words, had little clue of the extent of the enormous conflict between the fundamental principle of the democracy which they themselves advocated and the actual society in which they lived, a society that continued to reflect centuries of inequality ingrained from the past. Their lives contained both the democratic ideal and their acceptance of social practices that negated it. To the extent they accepted these practices, they were the enemy of the very ideal they sought to advance.

One of America's most important philosophers of democracy, Alexander Meiklejohn, recognized the ongoing nature of democratic growth. He acknowledged that "the Framers initiated a political revolution whose development is still in process throughout the world." But he also saw the Framers' limited vision. "The Framers could not foresee the specific issues which would arise as their 'novel idea' exercised its domination over the governing activities of a rapidly developing nation in a rapidly and fundamentally changing world. In that sense, the Framers did not know what they were doing. And in the same sense, it is still true that, after two centuries of experience, we do not know what they were doing, or what we ourselves are now doing."[3] Meiklejohn recognized that the assertion of the fundamental principle of democracy was only the beginning of an historical process that has not ended.

Thus, we must not look to the Founders for the full meaning of democracy, for they did not know. Those who think judges today should return to the "original" meaning of the Constitution are not advocates of democracy. Instead, we must look at the basic principles the Founders enunciated and continue the historical process of figuring out what these principles mean and how to strengthen and implement them in today's world.

The Founders' statement of the fundamental principle of democracy—the principle of equality—was only a start in the right direction. Just as *their* understanding of this principle was not fully developed, so must we assume that *our* understanding of it today may not be fully developed. While there has been considerable progress since the Declaration was written in 1776, we may still have a long way to go.

There is plenty of evidence that in the United States today the fundamental principle of democracy is far from being fully realized. It has taken more than 230 years to progress to where we are, but we must not become complacent, because our planet may not survive another decade if we continue down our current paths that include aggressive war and negligence toward the world's poor and the environment. Democratic values are still unfolding, and that unfolding is far from complete.

One of our biggest mistakes is to confuse the places we call "democracies" with the fulfillment of democratic values. "Democracies" and democratic values are not the same thing. Democratic values are the moral and ethical foundation upon which democracies rest. Democratic values constitute the moral and ethical goal to be achieved. Existing democracies are the incomplete and sometimes failed efforts to transform democratic values into social, political, and economic systems that convey those values.

As explained in Chapter 6, democratic values are logically tied to the "golden rule," when it is correctly understood to be a guide and not a "rule." This guide transcends any particular religion or nonreligious philosophy, for it is present in most of them. Like the "golden rule," democratic values express a moral and ethical goal, something continually to strive for no matter how often we fail to fully reach it. No existing democracy has reached the goal.

Any assumption that any existing democracy, such as the United States, represents the fulfillment of democratic values confuses the moral and ethical goal with what exists in fact. This confusion is dangerous. The confusion dilutes the goal by falsely assuming that the goal is fully reflected in the present state of things. This common confusion by Americans leads to complacency, a false sense of pride and arrogance, which, when combined with the nation's overwhelming economic and military power, makes the United States a potentially dangerous nation that too often does not hesitate to impose its will on other parts of the world, based on the false assumption that it fully represents the ideal to be achieved by others. The invasion of Iraq in 2003 is an example. But the ideal to be achieved is not well reflected in the present state of things and never has been.

Although we call it democracy, Americans live only in a partial democracy. The same is true for those living in other countries that are considered to be democracies. We do not yet know what a full democracy would be like. We are presumptuous, arrogant, and even ignorant to believe that we can impose democracy on other nations when we do not have it ourselves. As will become clear, the attempt to impose democracy on others is itself an expression of an anti-democratic mentality.

There are many examples of the enormous distance remaining between democratic values and the reality in the United States. Here are just a few examples, with more to follow later in this book.

Subversion of the Right to Vote

For eight years, 2000 - 2008, the United States lived under the presidency of George W. Bush. He was initially elected only because the right to vote was subverted. The relevant facts were widely known at the time, but the American public did little to protest. The public's complacency in the face of those facts reveals the ease with which democracy can falter.

The right to vote is widely thought to be the right to cast a ballot without barriers or intimidation. While this view is not false, it is too narrow. The right to vote is also a right to have all votes correctly counted in determining the outcome of an election. This did not happen in 2000 when Mr. Bush was elected to the presidency.

Without belittling the justifiable outrage expressed by many against the U.S. government's use of secret prisons around the world to hold people without trial, its use of torture, and its secret spying on U.S. citizens without court approval,[4] we must consider that it is the subversion of the right to vote that would most completely destroy democracy. The right of the public to vote follows from the recognition that the power of those in office does not give those in power greater worth. The people who choose through an election to give someone the power of a governmental office can also take away that power. Democratic values require that those in positions of power be accountable to the public. The electoral process, implementing the concept of "one person, one vote," is the primary means by which this can be achieved. But "one person, one vote" only works if all of the votes are correctly counted.

The national electoral process failed in the 2000 presidential election. Due to the closeness of that election nationally, the official vote in Florida determined the outcome for the nation. That vote in Florida deprived many of the right to vote. As one investigator concluded after a thorough study of the election in Florida, "[I]n any real, moral, and democratic sense, Al Gore should have been declared the victor over George W. Bush."[5] He further called the 2000 election of George W. Bush a "crime against democracy."[6] The crime was a crime not against any clear law but against the values of democracy. The U.S. Supreme Court ratified the crime.[7]

The failure of the electoral process in Florida in 2000 was not a one-time failure but a portent of the future. The flaws were structural. Our failure to correct the flaws is a continuing national failure. This failure due to our inaction is partly how we are the enemy of the values we profess.

In the 2000 presidential election, a disproportionate number of ethnic minorities were disenfranchised, mostly black and Jewish voters. It is their disenfranchisement by the thousands that caused Mr. Bush to be elected instead of Mr. Gore. Their disenfranchisement was not just their problem but the nation's problem that effectively disenfranchised every voter in the nation who voted for Mr. Gore.

A lengthy report by the U.S. Commission on Civil Rights titled "Voting Irregularities in Florida During the 2000 Presidential Election" documented that a purge list, purportedly designed to purge convicted felons from the voting rolls, contained the names of thousands of African-

Americans who were not convicted felons. The list was used to remove them, along with the felons, from the rolls of eligible voters. Given that over 80 percent of African-Americans voted for the Democratic candidate for president, Al Gore; that George W. Bush won the state of Florida by only 537 votes; and that the outcome in Florida determined who would be elected President of the United States, it is quite obvious that this purge list is what gave George W. Bush the presidency. There were many other problems as well that primarily disenfranchised African-American voters, without even considering the questionable practice of disenfranchising felons.[8]

African-Americans were not the only large minority group who were disenfranchised in Florida in 2000. In Florida's Palm Beach county, a largely Jewish population voted on a confusing ballot, resulting in approximately 3,000 or more votes intended for Al Gore going to Patrick Buchanan.[9] This by itself enabled George W. Bush to win the election. A badly designed ballot that confuses voters should invalidate an election, and a new election should have been held wherever that ballot had been used. But legal attempts to invalidate the ballots failed and the 3,000 votes were counted, contrary to the apparent intent of those voters.

The 2000 presidential election was not an anomaly. Democratic values crashed in 2000 and crashed again in the 2004 election. The official vote in Ohio determined the outcome of the 2004 presidential election. Numerous irregularities in Ohio in the 2004 election have been documented and confirmed. The correct outcome in Ohio in the 2004 presidential election remains in question given current evidence of the vast extent of the disenfranchisement of African-American voters. These irregularities included, among many other things, an insufficient number of voting machines in predominantly African-American areas, illegal restrictions on the use of provisional ballots that occurred more often in African-American areas, and actual intimidation of African-American voters.[10] These irregularities constituted a blatant violation of civil rights, reflecting what was typical in the Southern states prior to the civil rights movement.

Yet, nothing was done on a national level to correct the questionable outcome of the 2004 Ohio vote or to prevent repetition there or elsewhere. We turned a blind eye to these bad outcomes and have allowed future bad outcomes to continue. Thus, unless we make fundamental changes in national election law, these flawed voting processes will reoccur and change the outcome of elections.

These denials of the right to vote to thousands of Americans were a sabotage of democracy. The lack of opposition by the American public to this sabotage was complicity with it. Their complicity reflected a lack of concern about the values that form the basis of democracy. That we have not fixed the structural and legal flaws that caused these problems indicates the extent to which we are the enemy of the right to vote, a right that is essential to democracy and the values underlying it.

In contrast, in the autumn of 2004, when the people of Ukraine suspected an erroneous outcome of their election for president, hundreds of thousands of them in freezing weather peacefully took to the streets in Kiev and other cities and demanded a fair outcome. Their protest lasted for many days and successfully resulted in the Ukraine's Supreme Court ordering a new election. It is clear that the people of the Ukraine intensely cared about the outcome of their election. They took democracy seriously enough to take decisive but peaceful action when the votes were not correctly counted.

The new election changed the outcome.

With similar intensity, widespread protests erupted in Iran following the flawed national election in 2009. Unlike in Ukraine, the protesters faced death and imprisonment and were brutally suppressed. But the protesters showed that democracy mattered to them and that they were willing to face death to advance it.

The contrast of those events with the 2000 and 2004 presidential elections in the United States is discouragingly instructive. In the United States, the sabotaged national election of 2000 was openly protested only by a few thousand demonstrators in Washington, D.C.—an event not well reported at all—and by the relatively small African-American congressional delegation on the floor of the U.S. Senate.[11] No one took to the streets or did anything else in any significant numbers to protest the distorted 2004 presidential election in Ohio. Whereas in the Ukraine the defective election was replaced by a new election, in the United States, the idea of having a new election to replace a defective one is rarely expressed and often not legally possible. This is no small matter. The damage done under the eight years of the presidency of George W. Bush cost hundreds of thousands of Iraqi lives, ruined the lives of potentially innocent detainees, and left thousands of troops and civilians with life-long debilitating injuries. While this probably could not have been foreseen in 2000, it shows the critical importance of getting elections right and the consequences of indifference.

But to change the election laws faces both indifference and opposition. Winners of flawed elections usually want to make it difficult to review the results or to invalidate the elections. Thus, they ask for proof that the flaws were due to intentional, fraudulent acts or conspiracies before anything can be done to correct the flaws.[12] This is usually difficult to prove. Unfortunately the current law, as determined by the U.S. Supreme Court, weighs fully on the side of requiring direct proof of a discriminatory purpose to show any constitutional violations of voting rights.[13] This view requires showing that intentional wrongdoing caused the flawed elections instead of focusing on the flaws themselves. Accordingly, correcting the flaws becomes irrelevant unless wrongdoers can be found who intentionally caused the flaws. The law, so interpreted, cares little about getting correct results when flaws have been identified, unless someone can be found to blame. The law will not protect your right to vote if your vote is not counted, or if you are prevented from voting, unless you can find someone to blame and prove who intentionally did it.

Thus, the current legal framework that looks more to intentions than to results is a fundamental structural flaw in our electoral process. This national legal framework is not an adequate protection of our right to vote and have our votes count. We have to change the laws to protect democracy. Just as the Voting Rights Act of 1965 was needed to protect the voting rights of minorities, so will a new far-reaching national voting rights act be required to prevent continual repeats of what happened in Florida in 2000 and Ohio in 2004. There will continue to be uncorrected electoral failures if we continue to be complacent and do nothing about these structural flaws.

Although there is plenty of indication that the effective disenfranchisement of African-American voters in 2000 and 2004 was intentional, this should not matter and should not have to be proven. To say the election was sabotaged means that a significant flaw occurred in the voting process that very likely changed the outcome. Proof of intent should not be necessary. It has been firmly documented that thousands of

African-Americans were denied the right to vote in the 2000 and 2004 presidential elections and that over 80 percent of them were likely to vote for Mr. Bush's opponent.[14] It is obvious that these denials changed the outcome in Florida in 2000 and may have changed the outcome in Ohio in 2004. It was also obvious in the 2000 presidential election that Jewish voters of Palm Beach County, Florida, were effectively denied the right to vote. This denial alone changed the course of history and caused George W. Bush to be elected President of the United States.

Thus, even if no intentional acts of discrimination can be proven, the effect of denying several thousands of Americans the right to vote was itself enough to justify nullification of the 2000 presidential election in Florida and the 2004 election in Ohio. Nullifying an invalid election is what the people of Ukraine demanded when their election outcome appeared to have been sabotaged. That is what Iranian protesters sought in 2009 when the Iranian election appeared to have been sabotaged. That is what Americans would have demanded had they not been so complacent about democracy.

Discrimination against African-Americans, such as what occurred in the 2000 and 2004 presidential elections, is so ingrained in the society that it raised the eyebrows of only a few. And then for many it was only their eyebrows that were raised, as they slumbered back on their couches to watch some television show far removed from the political and social reality that affects us daily. I do not say this lightly: the apathy in the United States is appalling. Only 55.3 percent of voting-age U.S. citizens voted in the 2004 presidential election, and only 37 percent voted in the federal elections of 2002. The percentage of those voting is usually even much lower in local elections. Our apathy as a nation is pathetic and continues.

This apathy has allowed the use of certain kinds of

electronic voting machines that cannot be known to record votes correctly, verify the votes, or be reliably secured.[15] In 2006, six years after the Florida fiasco, electronic voting machines failed to record an estimated 18,000 votes in an important congressional election.[16] Similar machines made it impossible to verify the outcome of a very close election held in November 2007 in Cuyahoga County, Ohio. In the presidential primary elections of 2007, an estimated one-third of the votes were cast on similar unreliable machines, and many of them were used in the presidential election of 2008.[17] The use of such machines is a direct and effective assault on democracy. They are still in use in many places.

But, on a national level, we have not cared enough to correct this assault. We also do not sufficiently realize that the denial of the right to vote to anyone, regardless of ethnicity, is a denial affecting all. If you vote for a candidate, you expect all of the votes for that candidate to be counted, not just your own vote. The failure to count someone else's vote for the person you voted for effectively nullifies your vote. In this sense, the failure to count the legitimate vote of one is a denial of the right to vote for all.

To protect democratic values, the legal framework pertaining to elections needs to change. The fundamental principle of democracy does not mean that your right to vote can be enforced only if it can be proven that it was intentionally denied. The fundamental principle of democracy does not mean that your equality can be disregarded unless it can be proven that someone intentionally disregarded it. The right to vote and to have your vote and everyone's vote counted is independent of anyone's intention. No conspiracy or fraud needs to be proven. If that right has been denied on a wide scale, for whatever reason sufficient to throw into question the outcome of an election, that election should be declared void and a new election declared. If the law does not provide for a new election, then the law is flawed and must be changed if democracy is to prevail.

Continuing Past Prejudice

Consider, too, other examples showing that American democracy is at best in its adolescence. While we may think that women are closer than ever to being treated as equal to men, there is still no equal rights amendment in the U.S. Constitution guaranteeing equal rights to women. The currently proposed Equal Rights Amendment provides, "Equality of rights under law shall not be denied or abridged by the United States or by any state on account of sex." It was approved by Congress in 1972, but only 35 of the needed 38 states have ratified it. In a country that proclaims itself to be a democracy, how is it that decades later fifteen states have not ratified an amendment guaranteeing equal rights for women? Clearly a substantial part of the United States will not affirmatively support the principle that all people are created equal.

The rights of others are also in jeopardy. A national survey conducted in October and November of 2004 revealed a widespread desire to limit the rights of Americans who are Muslims. Forty-four percent of voting age Americans polled, in a study conducted at Cornell University, supported restricting the civil liberties of Muslim Americans.[18] Such support reflects blatant discrimination based on religion and perhaps also reflects an underlying racism combined with ignorance about Muslim Americans. Clearly, a substantial minority of Americans either do not know what democratic values are, do not understand them, or do not support them.

Even more shocking was that this same survey found that

63 percent of the respondents believe that the government should be able to detain *suspected* terrorists indefinitely.[19] This large majority of respondents does not even recognize a fundamental principle contained in the Bill of Rights, which guarantees due process of law. *Anyone can be "suspected."* "Suspected terrorists" who are detained indefinitely, such as occurred in Guantanamo, did not get due process of law. It is only one short step to detaining "suspected terrorists" who may be doing nothing more than exercising their constitutional right to speak freely and criticize government policy. It is only another short step to detaining anyone profiled as a "suspected terrorist" who fits predefined cultural criteria programmed into a computer, creating a new form of racist-like behavior based on computerized profiles. Every time we do not stand up for the rights of the accused, including "suspected terrorists," we are the enemy of democratic values.

Another example: Much of the nation is still not ready to give same-gender couples rights equal to heterosexual couples. In 2008, 43 states had laws banning same-gender marriages (with no option for "civil unions"), and most of these states had the bans incorporated into their state constitutions. Consequently, gays should be considered an oppressed group in most states, a group without equal rights. Even in those few states where state law seeks to give same-gender couples rights equal to heterosexual couples, many private companies still discriminate against same-gender couples in providing employee benefits.[20] In most of the rest of the United States, same-gender couples are not even legally recognized, and in many places they are in danger of being physically assaulted. This is a denial of equal rights.

The death penalty is another blatant denial of the principle that all people are created equal. To take a life intentionally for any reason other than to prevent another's death is a denial of the equal worth of every human life. Instead, the death penalty is an expression of an undemocratic principle that effectively says your equal worth as a human being is not inherent but instead depends on whether we think you deserve it.

American Nationalism

In addition—and even more critical in today's global environment—American nationalism assumes that the life of a United States citizen is worth more than the life of anyone else. The United States is a particularly nationalistic place, particularly during the 2000 – 2008 Bush administration when the President designated certain other nations as "evil." He led the majority of the public and Congress to accept the idea that it is all right to invade another sovereign nation to protect American interests, even when the victimized nation, like Iraq, had no realistic ability to conquer another nation. Just as when the United States tried to control Vietnam—a terrible venture that failed and left horrendous devastation in its wake—in Iraq we hear a frequent count of total American lives lost but infrequently of totals of Iraqi civilian lives lost. By many estimates, many tens of thousands of Iraqis have died, likely hundreds of thousands, mostly innocent women, children, and noncombatant men, as a consequence of the U.S. invasion. According to one estimate reported in October 2004, in the early stages of the war 100,000 Iraqis had died as a consequence of the war, including those who died due to indirect consequences such as the loss of infrastructure.[21] As of the summer of 2005, an estimated 25,000 civilians and nonmilitary personnel had been directly killed, over 9,000 of whom were killed by U.S.-led forces.[22] Even then President

George W. Bush stated—without remorse—in response to a question on December 12, 2005, "How many Iraqi citizens have died in this war? I would say 30,000, more or less, have died as a result of the initial incursion and the ongoing violence against Iraqis."[23]

But as the war has unfolded, many more have died. In November of 2006, Iraqi's Health Minister, Ali al-Shemari, estimated that 150,000 civilians had been killed in the war.[24] In October of 2006, the British medical journal *Lancet* estimated that 600,000 Iraqis have died of war-related violence since the U.S. invasion.[25] The number of Iraqis who have died as an aftermath of the U.S. invasion, directly from violence and indirectly from destroyed infrastructure, is probably now so huge that it cannot be reasonably estimated.

While most of the news media occasionally report the total number of American military personnel killed in Iraq, it is rare to see any coverage of the total loss of Iraqi civilian lives, which is many times greater. As far as the American news media are concerned, one American life seems to be more valuable than many more Iraqi lives. As one commentator stated, "In Iraq we kill off thousands, perhaps tens of thousands of innocent civilians with our own hands, and we reject any attempt to comprehend what we have done."[26] When we think this way, we do not practice democracy. We do not practice the principle that all people are created equal, that all people are of equal worth. People who are different, particularly if they are not U.S. citizens, are devalued, inferior at best and evil at worst. This is a denial of democratic values.

We do not practice democratic values unless we experience the loss of each Iraqi life, whether a combatant or a civilian, as vividly and with the same horror and sorrow as we feel the loss of an American soldier or civilian. This is what the principle of equality means and requires.

Are we ready to embrace this consequence of democratic values?

Comprehending the Extent of Our Failure and Progress

It is fair to say that if we affirm the idea of democracy but accept these ills, we are either misinformed or hypocritical. The same charge can be made toward the Founders, who called Native Americans "merciless Indian savages" in the very same Declaration of Independence that proclaimed that all men are created equal.

Nonetheless, their hypocrisy or ignorance—and ours— does not diminish the power and value of the principle they professed and we profess: *All people are created equal.* We are imperfect beings who have high ideals that we strive for but fail to attain. That does not mean that the ideals are flawed, only that we are flawed. The ideal is sound. The goal remains to be attained.

As a nation, Americans have even made considerable progress toward attaining this ideal since 1776. Slavery has been banned. Killing a Native American is murder whereas before, particularly in the nineteenth century, killing Native Americans was an encouraged sport. Married women are no longer the legal property of their husbands. Civil rights laws have been passed, effectively abolishing legal apartheid (though the practice of apartheid is still quite evident, and its effects were quite apparent during the partial evacuation of New Orleans in 2005 as Hurricane Katrina devastated the area). The voting rights of minorities are now legally protected even though the laws are still inadequate. A few states now recognize that same-gender couples can have the same rights and privileges as married different-gender couples, though it will probably be a very long time before most other states join them. In 2008, the voters of the United States elected a person of mixed African and white ancestry to be President, a vote that was a public repudiation of the racism of the past.

Thus, just as we have numerous examples of America's failure to be a democracy, we also have numerous examples of a long, hard struggle toward fulfilling the democratic ideal. But we must not let our progress blind us to the fact that we still have a very long way to go. It is doubtful we are even halfway there.

Recognizing the vast chasm between democratic values and our current reality is critical to understanding what those values are. If we are blind to the chasm, we effectively diminish democratic values by assuming that they are essentially equivalent to the way things are today. If we make that mistake, we will never comprehend what democratic values are and what they mean.

As a nation, we allowed President Bush to lead us astray— as is examined in more detail in Chapter 3. He did so, in part, by portraying the United States as the ideal to be attained. Accordingly, the United States could do no wrong. But by invading Iraq, the United States tried to impose democracy on others by force, an idea that denies the equality of the human targets of this force. The invasion was a denial of democracy in the name of democracy, an assault on democracy in its name.

If we could have been so easily led astray, what will prevent a similar error in the future?

The Paradox of Democracy

We must come to terms with the paradox of democracy.

The paradox of democracy is that the life of each person who is against democracy is equal in value to the life of each person who favors democracy. Those who are against democracy are not "evil." They must have the same rights and privileges— and responsibilities toward others—as those who favor democracy. The paradox of democracy is a direct consequence of the fundamental principle of democracy, that all people are created equal *regardless of their views and practices.*

The 2003 invasion of Iraq demonstrated ignorance of this paradox. Instead of "all people are created equal," the United States said, in effect, "All people who believe in democracy are created equal. The rest we can oppress, imprison or kill until they change their ways." From unnecessarily dropping two atomic bombs on major population centers in Japan to the history of controlling or attempting to control many of the governments of Latin America and the Middle East to the invasion of Vietnam to the invasion of Iraq, the United States has in the past done just that, in excessive abundance.[27]

How can we continually perpetuate such a blatant contradiction between what we say we believe and what we do? How can we be certain we will not again regress into anti-democratic ways?

Getting to the Source of the Problem

The answer is not simple. It is not simply stupidity. It is not merely a moral failing. It is not that we are bad or evil. The problem is much more complex and difficult to solve.

The problem lies deeply within our individual and collective psyches. The problem is that after over two centuries of proclaiming the democratic ideal, we—along with most of the rest of the world—still often think in accordance with an ancient pre-democratic morality that is thousands of years old. This pre-democratic morality lies in our unconscious and is passed on from generation to generation without awareness. To fulfill democratic values, we must become aware of what this pre-democratic morality is and begin conscious work toward replacing this ancient morality with democratic values. The next chapter will explain what this ancient morality is.

This does not mean that we should attack those who express this ancient pre-democratic morality. We carry anti-democratic views *within ourselves.* It is everywhere we go. As one book's title pointed out, "wherever you go, there you are." When Americans invaded Iraq, we carried some of these anti-democratic values with us and imposed them on others with every gunshot, missile launch, and bomb. If we were trying to get rid of anti-democratic ways, we might have done as well to shoot ourselves. But that is not the solution either, for, after all, our lives are just as precious as those of others.

Instead, we must identify the offending anti-democratic ways and replace them—within ourselves as well as in our social and political environment—with democratic values. This requires that we *carefully examine and change the way we think.* When the way we think is anti-democratic, the way we act will be anti-democratic.

This does not mean, however, that we refrain from social action until we perfect our thoughts. It is a fallacy to think that social change must come *after* personal change. Societal and personal practices interact. Social practices, institutions and our surrounding culture embody many anti-democratic practices. They affect us and impede personal change. Personal change must include working to change anti-democratic practices wherever we see them. In the process we come to understand better what democratic values mean as we put them into practice, targeting for change not only ourselves but also the local, national and world communities we live in.

Thus, as we seek to change ourselves, we cannot do this effectively in isolation from one another. We must help each other do it, with generosity of spirit, humor and forgiveness. In addition, we must work together to identify the anti-democratic practices in our surroundings and change them. We cannot get far as isolated individuals trying to perfect our inner being.

We also must not divert energy from the task ahead by punishing ourselves for our own failures. Instead, we have to work with each other, respecting each other as equals, in the long-term process of replacing anti-democratic social practices with ones that better embody democratic values. In other words, we have to live democratic values in our own lives as we seek to spread them.

In this process we will actively support social policies and political candidates who also support the creating of a more democratic society while respecting the paradox of democracy. At times, we may have to be more active and follow the good example of the people of Ukraine in 2004, reflecting at least the active enthusiasm for democracy that they showed then as we also explore other means of effective social change that go beyond protest.

By working together and putting into practice the ideal of the equality of worth of all human beings, we can help get the United States back on the right track where it might become a leader that others will want to follow instead of a powerful world tyrant imposing its will on others through threats, economic control and military violence. We can advance democratic values by thinking and practicing them wherever we are, anywhere in the world, including engaging in social and political action. In short, we can stop being our enemy and become the friend and supporter of the values we hold and profess.

But to do this we need a greater understanding of what democratic values consist of and how they conflict with the anti-democratic mentality persisting from the vast undemocratic past of humankind.

Chapter 2

How We Learn and Sustain An Anti-Democratic Mentality

> *Democratic values override traditional and commonly accepted beliefs about "good" and "evil."*

Like the Founders, we carry within ourselves unresolved conflicts between democratic values and persisting age-old anti-democratic ways of thinking and behavior. These anti-democratic traditions and paradigms feed and sustain an anti-democratic mentality. This anti-democratic mentality is still very prevalent in the nations we now call "democracies." Seeing and overcoming the conflict between this anti-democratic mentality and democratic values is difficult but necessary if we are advance democracy. Like the early abolitionists, we must look ahead to what democracy should be, based on democratic values, and identify and reject the anti-democratic ways of thinking and behavior that are present in the culture.

If we are to see and overcome this conflict between democratic values and this anti-democratic mentality, we must understand what this mentality consist of, including its history and present influence, and also have a clear understanding of what democratic values should mean in our daily lives.

How Our Undemocratic Past Influences Us

We all are guided by ideas, paradigms and beliefs instilled in us from birth that we often do not think about or question. Usually we just accept them, without awareness, as given truths and live accordingly. They become mental habits and beliefs that affect how we live and think. We are unlikely to realize fully what these mental habits and beliefs are or how they affect us unless we choose to reflect, inquire and question. Many of these mental habits and beliefs, handed down from generation to generation, stem from our undemocratic past when hierarchical class structures and established authority were not questioned. Thus, many of these mental habits and beliefs are persisting, long-lasting carry-overs from our long undemocratic past and the undemocratic past of most of humankind.

Since this undemocratic past, and not democratic values, has dominated most of human history, we continually struggle to replace this extensive undemocratic past with democratic values. This struggle has not fully succeeded even in countries called "democracies." The undemocratic past of humankind persists in many of our learned mental habits and beliefs that often operate beneath consciousness.

Thus, while we may consciously believe in democratic values, undemocratic mental habits and beliefs have nonetheless been instilled in us from birth by our social and cultural surroundings. These surroundings include our parents, who received the beliefs and mental habits of their parents who received them from their parents, and so on. Unless we persistently probe and question what we have been taught and think about the meaning of democratic values, we pass these same mental habits and beliefs on to our children, just as previous parents have done.

Because these mental habits and beliefs are often unconscious, we sustain them inadvertently. To be effective in changing these mental habits and beliefs, we should focus on moving forward and not, instead, on blaming our parents or ourselves. Becoming aware of these habits and beliefs is an essential first step toward moving forward and overcoming their control over our lives.

The reason these mental habits and beliefs are important is that they guide how we live, both as individuals and collectively as a society. When the social norm was to accept slavery, the attempts of slaves to gain freedom were viciously punished. When the social norm was to see women as the property of their husbands, a husband could rape his wife who would have no legal recourse. These were the norms when the Founders proclaimed that all men are created equal, and they remained the norms for many decades afterwards. These norms were nothing more than the mental habits and beliefs handed down from one generation to the next. These mental habits and beliefs sustained and supported tyrannies over slaves and women—in conflict with democratic values.

Thus, tyrannies do not exist through coercive power alone. They exist because large numbers of people, usually including even the victims of tyrannies, tacitly accept these tyrannies as justifiable based on their own beliefs. It was the clear expression of a new belief in human equality, as expressed at the beginning of the Declaration of Independence, that inspired and energized the American Revolution in 1776. The victory of the revolution also depended on a successful military defense against military repression, but it was a change of beliefs that ultimately led to the revolution's success. Similarly, it will be a change of our beliefs that will enable us to live more fully in accordance with democratic values.

When we see the many components of anti-democratic mentality, we may be surprised to see not only that they are widely accepted by *others*, but also that we too accept them in varying degrees. To understand these anti-democratic mental habits and beliefs is to recognize within ourselves conflicts that we may not have fully resolved. In short, a major enemy of democratic values is not "out there" to be conquered by force, but the mental habits and beliefs that lie within us.

How to Identify Anti-Democratic Mentality

Anti-democratic mentality consists of the mental habits, beliefs, ways of thinking, views, perspectives, concepts and assumptions that express or support the idea that some people's lives are worth more than the lives of others. This mentality usually includes the view that some people are so bad or evil that they should be killed.

Popular stories and entertainment often contribute to an anti-democratic mentality. They commonly portray the battles of good against evil, where evil is not just as a set of bad actions or beliefs but is embodied in a person or group that deserves to be killed. In movies, novels, and children's stories, the evil ones are killed, and we cheer their deaths. They are the witches, the evil magicians, the demonic. The message is that certain people are not created equal; they are evil, so we should kill them, or if they die inadvertently, we should celebrate. This message (like that of *Hansel and Gretel*) is all around us.

Historically, anti-democratic views have pervaded most of the world and continue to do so today. An anti-democratic mentality and democratic values coexist in all of the countries called "democracies." The death penalty could not exist without the anti-democratic mentality that supports it. An anti-democratic mentality may be found in liberals, conservatives, those on the left, right, and in the middle. Most of us, probably all of us, have within ourselves a mixture of democratic values and an anti-democratic mentality; thus, we are inconsistent, conflicted and frequently confused. As a result, many of us express anti-democratic ideas in the name of democracy and inadvertently not only help give democracy a bad name but also destroy the very things we want to protect.

But we cannot live consistently in accordance with democratic values if an anti-democratic mentality is mixed with democratic values. We cannot effectively advance democratic values if we are confused and advance anti-democratic ways of thinking while believing that we are expressing the values of democracy.

A key thing to remember is this: *the difference between democratic values and an anti-democratic mentality is that democratic values mean that the worth of a person is not dependent on what that person believes.* To affirm democratic values we must also affirm that people who express anti-democratic ways of thinking are of equal worth as those who hold democratic values. Having an anti-democratic mentality, consciously or inadvertently, does not make anyone a bad or evil person. That a person believes something we may regard as wrong or evil does not make the holder of that belief evil. Even those who believe what we despise are nonetheless human beings equal to ourselves.

If we remember this paradox of democracy, we will see how democratic values are fundamentally different from an anti-democratic mentality.

How Moralistic Dualism Sustains an Anti-Democratic Mentality

Anti-democratic mentality is the result of *moralistic dualism*, a way of thinking that divides people into good and bad. Moralistic dualism classifies people as more or less worthy depending on how good or bad we think they are. It implies that some people are so unworthy that they deserve to die. It presumes we can make that judgment and know who is good and who is not and who should live and who should die.

The fact that most people share these ideas in varying degrees illustrates the prevalence of anti-democratic ways of thinking within the culture. These ways of thinking are still with us because of the long and honored tradition of moralistic dualism. Moralistic dualism has been used throughout the history of humankind to justify and sustain undemocratic societies. But this prevalent and long-standing tradition must not blind us from seeing that moralistic dualism utterly conflicts with the idea that all people are of equal worth.

In its strongest and most prevalent form, moralistic dualism embraces the metaphysical belief that a force of Evil exists in the universe. It is this Evil that is presumed, often unconsciously, to invade people's inner being and make them inalterably evil. This view leads those who believe in it to proclaim that infidels should be killed and evil empires invaded and overthrown regardless of the cost to human life.

Fundamentalist versions of most religions rely on moralistic dualism to separate the believers from the unbelievers and the faithful from the heretics. These religious sects attract believers with promises of heavenly rewards and strike into their hearts fear of the unbelievers who are portrayed as evil people who would destroy the believers if not stopped.

But it is not just fundamentalist versions of religion that advance moralistic dualism. For well over two millennia, famous philosophers and theologians have equated moralistic dualism with morality itself. For them and their followers, not to believe in the known forces of good and evil is at best a result of ignorance and at worst is a despicable form of agnosticism or heresy.

Once a person is caught up in moralistic dualism, it becomes difficult to escape, because the believer becomes good and anyone who disagrees becomes bad. The believer then becomes surrounded by a mental wall of assumed goodness that rejects criticism as bad. This wall is the mental trap of moralistic dualism. This trap is possibly why moralistic dualism has dominated the history of humankind and is so difficult to eradicate. It is a trap that has captured the most revered philosophers and theologians as well as the young soldiers who sacrifice themselves in the name of God, country and "freedom."

Thus, moralistic dualism is not merely a mental belief residing in our heads. It is a paradigm that structures how we think and feel about other people and how we act toward them. It is often backed up by governmental power that suppresses and punishes dissent. People who are not convicted of anything specific are imprisoned, tortured and executed because of it. Not too long ago, in the United States the evil targets were called "communists." Today they are called "terrorists" and "suspected terrorists." To attack the evil ones, we wage war and build arsenals of weapons that could destroy the earth. Soldiers and innocent civilians die because of these beliefs. Moralistic dualism is what supports our belief that we are right to kill, and it encourages us to feel good when certain people are killed. It also provides imagined moral support for nations considered to be democracies to imprison and torture suspects without trial, spy on anyone and everyone, and ignore the right of privacy.

Moralistic dualism does not allow that there is a difference between doing what is necessary to protect ourselves and others from harm and believing that the harm is caused by evil people.

The Honored Tradition of Moralistic Dualism[28]

Moralistic dualism has a long and influential history that we still honor today. The advocates of moralistic dualism include the glorified "great men" of Western religious and intellectual history, such as Plato, Aristotle, St. Augustine, Martin Luther, John Calvin, Immanuel Kant and Sigmund Freud. *These thinkers were opposed to democracy. Their exalted and elaborate ways of thinking provided the ideological support for undemocratic societies.* They viewed themselves as the elite and disparaged those from lower classes, other cultures or religions, and the opposite gender.

Our ability to detect anti-democratic ways of thinking within ourselves will be greatly aided if we understand what these lauded men taught and believed, since their influence extends into the present and will continue into the future. We must continue to study them and their influences, but critically from the perspective of democratic values, not as the wonderful ideas of great men as is common even today. (Although I limit myself here to a "Western" inquiry, parallels can be found all over the world where ancient heroes and honored figures not only did not advocate democratic values but openly opposed them.)

What better way to advance undemocratic societies than to conceive of the entire universe as hierarchically structured, with human societies arranged to reflect the universal structure? This is exactly what these great men did, in varying ways. What is common to them is the moralistic view of the universal hierarchy, with the Good or God or Reason at the top of the hierarchy and increasingly bad things below. People are seen as being distributed vertically within the universal hierarchy. Those at the top are seen as good. Those at the bottom are seen as people who should be enslaved, imprisoned or killed. Such images of the hierarchical distribution of people conflict with democracy.

Such conceptions of an idealized hierarchical order are age-old and thoroughly ingrained in over twenty-three centuries of tradition.[29] An idealized hierarchically structured universe was advanced in a clear form by Plato (427? - 347 BCE), who is perhaps the most influential philosopher in Western history. His famous hierarchical analogy of the "Divided Line" and his "Allegory of the Cave" illustrated an eternal hierarchy of Good and not-Good. The Good lies at the top of the vertical Divided Line and is defined as unchangeable forms knowable only through the intellect. He contrasted intellectual knowledge of the Good with sensory awareness, which he placed toward the bottom of the Divided Line. The senses, bodily feeling and emotion pull us in a direction downward, opposite to that leading upwards toward the Good. Since the mass of humankind is governed by the senses, emotion and bodily feeling, they are trapped at the bottom, far away from the Good and thus are not capable of ruling themselves or of participating in their governance. The rulers must come from an intellectual elite, referred to as philosopher-kings, for only they have the intellectual skills necessary to apprehend the Good.

In Plato's view, all people are not of equal worth. Some must be slaves. Members of the general public must not determine their destinies or that of their society. Determining the destiny of society is reserved for the philosopher-kings. Plato's portrayal of a hierarchical universe was his justification for deploring democracy and advancing rule by a small elite.[30]

Plato's philosophy set the stage on which much of "Western" intellectual development has played for over two millennia. As two prominent scholars noted, "The late Professor Alfred North Whitehead was barely exaggerating when he said that the development of Western philosophy has been largely a matter of adding footnotes to Plato."[31] In comparison with this twenty-three to twenty-four centuries-old tradition of hierarchy, democracy in the form of government as we know it today is still a preadolescent, born of ideas a little over 300 years old.[32]

Plato's famous pupil, Aristotle (384 - 322 BCE), provided the first major footnote. He too taught that the rulers of society should be an intellectual elite. Like Plato, he taught that the mind is superior to the bodily senses and asserted that those who exercise the mind should be the rulers of society. "For that which can foresee by the exercise of mind is by nature intended to be lord and master, and that which can with its body give effect to such foresight is a subject, and by nature a slave."[33] The intellectual elite is generally determined by birth: "For that some should rule and others be ruled is a thing not only necessary, but expedient; from the hour of their birth, some are marked out for subjection, others for rule."[34] Obviously, Aristotle opposed democracy. Similarly to Plato, Aristotle thought it was "obvious" that some people should be slaves.

Many famous Christian theologians advanced moralistic dualism, often in extreme forms. St. Augustine (354 - 430 CE) wrote another major footnote to Plato, bringing Christianity onto the Platonic stage and replacing the intellect that Plato put at the top of his Divided Line with Christian faith. He left intact the bottom of Plato's Divided Line, referring to sensory awareness as derived from the sinful "flesh." Thus, for St. Augustine, the Good (God) is attained through Christian faith, and those who do not have such faith are governed by the sinful body, the flesh, and the sensory experiences lying at the bottom of the Divided Line. Only the faithful can overcome the flesh. Those who are not faithful are necessarily sinful and evil.

Much of Christian doctrine which followed adopted these elements of Augustinian theology—a theology that divides humankind into the faithful believers and sinful nonbelievers. According to this tradition, the sinful are unworthy. Only the believers are worthy. There is no room here for equality between the believers and the nonbelievers.

Martin Luther (1483 - 1546) and John Calvin (1509 - 1564) continued this tradition of distinguishing faith from the flesh, the former being good, the latter sinful and evil. Martin Luther made it clear that there are good people, defined by their faith, and bad people. "We must divide the children of Adam and all mankind into two classes, the first belonging to the kingdom of God, the second to the kingdom of the world. Those who belong to the kingdom of God are all the true believers who are in Christ and under Christ."[35] He used vehement war-like terms to say what should happen to the bad people: "The sword can have no place among Christians; therefore, you cannot bear it among Christians or hold it over them, for they do not need it. . . . To the other group, the non-Christians . . . the other proposition applies . . . you are under obligation to serve and assist the sword by whatever means you can, with body, goods, honor, and soul."[36] John Calvin was equally disdainful of the non-Christians: "All who are estranged from the religion of the one God, however admirable they may be regarded on account of their reputation for virtue, not only deserve no reward but rather punishment, because by the pollution of their hearts they defile God's good works."[37]

Thus, you have in these historically respected Christian theologians a clear advocacy of moralistic dualism: The worthy people are defined by their faith; the unworthy by their lack of faith. Since the unworthy are not equal to the worthy, the idea of human equality is denied. Since democracy rests on the concept of human equality, the views of these theologians are incompatible with democracy.[38]

Furthermore, these views supported aggression against those considered unworthy. Whatever may be said about the economic or material causes of imperialism and colonialism, these deeds were encouraged and supported by the ideology of moralistic dualism. Whether moralistic dualism or greed came first does not matter; they often go together and sustain each other. These famous philosophers and theologians of the past, wittingly or not, provided the value structure that could readily be used to justify forcibly taking over other lands and conquering other peoples.

The famous philosopher Immanuel Kant (1724 - 1804) reaffirmed the Platonic reliance on reason as the path to the Good. He encapsulated his view of the Good into his moral maxims. Like his noted predecessors, he treated feeling and sensory awareness as pulling us away from knowledge of morality. Most people, in his view, are unable to free themselves from sensory awareness and are not capable of disciplining themselves to engage in the kind of reasoning that leads to the Good. "Undisciplined men are apt to follow every caprice. We see this also among savage nations, who, though they may discharge functions for some time like Europeans, yet can never become accustomed to European manners. With them, however, it is not the noble love of freedom which Rousseau and others imagine, but a kind of barbarism—the animal, so to speak, not having yet developed its human nature."[39] The undisciplined should be controlled by the disciplined. "In order to bring either an as yet uneducated or a degraded mind into the path of the morally good, some preparatory guidance is needed to attract it by a view to its own advantage or to frighten it by fear of harm."[40] Since any society includes a majority of those who do not measure up to Kant's view of worthiness, it is not surprising that he spoke against democracy, calling it a form of "despotism."[41]

Sigmund Freud (1856 - 1939) was very much a Kantian in his way of thinking about humankind's higher achievements and the proper rulers of society and even the world. For Freud, civilization is advanced through the use of reason to renounce instinct. Since only a minority are capable of the mental discipline required for this renunciation, that minority should rule. "It is just as impossible to do without control of the mass by a minority as it is to dispense with coercion in the work of civilization. For the masses are lazy and unintelligent; they have no love for instinctual renunciation."[42] Thus, in his view, coercion of the masses by an elite is required to advance civilization. In this respect, Freud's view added another footnote to Plato.

For over two millennia, from Plato through Freud, we see a

hierarchical dividing line that places the Good or God at the top reached either through reason or faith, with sensory awareness, instinct, emotion and feeling at the bottom. This vertical line, in turn, has been linked to people who reflect the various positions on this line. Those considered the most worthy are those closest to the Good or God. Those considered least worthy are furthest from the Good or God. The famous thinkers who proclaimed these views reasoned that just as the bad should be subordinated and controlled by the good, so should those less worthy be subordinated and controlled by those who are more worthy. Whether the worthy are defined in terms of their intellectual capacities, rational discipline, renunciation of instinct, or faith, they are seen as the proper rulers: It is they who should control the unworthy, using coercion whenever they think it is needed.

This long, respected and honored tradition rejects democratic values. It asserts that all people are not of equal worth. To affirm the values of democracy, we must recognize this tradition for what it is, an elaborate rationale for undemocratic social control by an elite. It is a rationale that supports hierarchically ruled societies and the use of coercion to control the masses.

If we are to advance democratic values, we must cease conveying this anti-democratic history as part of the great tradition of Western culture. Western culture has changed and moved toward democracy, based on a different tradition that has developed gradually. Those advocating democracy have, in effect, rejected the tradition of Plato through Freud in favor of another vision of a good society, a society that acknowledges the equal worth of every human being. But we must also recognize the extent to which the ideal society envisioned by Plato and his intellectual descendents is still a part of our mentality and still interferes with our progress toward greater democracy.

How Moralistic Dualism Sustains Racism and the Inequality of Women

Throughout its history, moralistic dualism has been used to justify the oppression of women by associating them with the sensory and emotional awareness that lies toward the bottom of Plato's Divided Line. The thinkers espousing these views generally saw the top of the hierarchy as populated mostly or exclusively by men like themselves.

Women are among the most notable and consistent historical victims of moralistic dualism. Though they constitute approximately one-half of any society, the teachings of moralistic dualism generally assign them to the bottom of the social hierarchy where they are categorized similarly to the men engaged in physical labor.

Among these lauded thinkers we have discussed above, only Plato expressed the idea that women might join men as leaders or rulers of society.[43] But he also said, "The greatest number and variety of desires and pleasures and pains is generally to be found in children and women and slaves, and in the less respectable majority of so-called free men."[44] With this one sentence, Plato summed up the dominant attitude toward women held by these famous men and their followers.

Aristotle, for example, relegated women to a completely subservient position. He said, "The male is by nature superior, and the female inferior; and the one rules, and the other is ruled; this principle, of necessity, extends to all mankind." "The male is by nature fitter for command than the female, just as the elder and full-grown is superior to the younger and more immature." "The courage of a man is shown in commanding, of a woman, in obeying."[45]

St. Augustine affirmed quotations from I Corinthians 7: "A man does well to abstain from all commerce with women." "He who is unmarried is concerned with God's claim, asking how he is to please God; whereas the married man is concerned with the world's claim, asking how he is to please his wife."[46] The historical purpose of celibacy, given that only men could assume high positions of leadership, is to prevent women from polluting the connection of these men to God.

While Protestants generally do not advocate celibacy, historically dominant Protestant leaders supported the idea that women must be subordinate to men. Martin Luther said, "A wife ought to be obedient to her husband as her lord, be subject to him, yield to him, keep silent and agree with him as long as it is not contrary to God."[47] John Calvin said, "Wives cannot obey Christ unless they yield obedience to their husbands."[48] For them, intimacy with women was acceptable, but only as long as the women were married and subordinate to their husbands.

Immanuel Kant proclaimed, "The fair sex has just as much understanding as the male, but it is a beautiful understanding, whereas ours should be a deep understanding, an expression that signifies identity with the sublime."[49] Kant goes on to insult the intellect of women: "A woman who has a head full of Greek . . . or carries on fundamental controversies about mechanics . . . might as well even have a beard. . . . A woman therefore will learn no geometry. . . . Her philosophy is not to reason, but to sense. . . . I hardly believe that the fair sex is capable of principles. . . ."[50] Clearly, if unable to have principles, women, in his view, are not fit to govern.

Sigmund Freud reaffirmed the insult. "Women soon come into opposition to civilization and display their retarding and restraining influence. . . . The work of civilization has become increasingly the business of men, it confronts them with ever more difficult tasks and compels them to carry out instinctual sublimations of which women are little capable."[51] But women cause little harm as long as she "choose[s] her husband for his paternal characteristics and . . . recognize[s] his authority."[52]

In each case, these lauded thinkers assigned women to the lower half of Plato's Divided Line, asserting that women's sensuality, desire, passion, feelings, and instincts prevent them from the higher intellectual achievements of which only a few men are capable.

Just as they assigned women to "lower" human experiences, so did they also assign men of other "races" or ethnicities. Sigmund Freud summed up and affirmed a long-standing justification for racism: "Leadership of the human species" has fallen upon the "great ruling powers among the white nations."[53] At the bottom of the social hierarchy are "primitive" people who cannot control their instincts. Among the "primitive" peoples Freud named the "Negro races of Africa," the Melanesian, Polynesian, and Malayan peoples, and the native people of Australia and North and South America.[54] Freud viewed the nonwhite peoples of the world similarly to the way he viewed women—as people not capable of controlling their instincts and who therefore should be ruled by those who can.

Perhaps today Freud and his predecessors are "turning over in their graves" as women and nonwhites assume more positions of leadership and power. But the views of these great men of the past have not disappeared and instead persist all over the world, including in nations we call "democracies."

The way of thinking that ranks people by their closeness to or distance from some preconceived notion of the "Good" is what constitutes moralistic dualism. This way of thinking asserts that some people are more worthy than others and morally superior, because they are closer to the "Good." Thus, they should rule. Others should be ruled because of their moral inferiority. We can identify the morally superior either by their intellect or faith (depending on which version of moralistic dualism is believed). We can identify the morally inferior by their closeness to sensory experience, their bodies, emotion and feeling, or to nature. When, as in Freud's view, the morally inferior include all women, all non-whites, and the masses of whites who cannot control their instincts, we are left with only small elite of white males who should control the world.

But regardless of what one sees as the "Good" at the top of the hierarchy or who one sees as the most worthy, *the problem is the undemocratic structure of the hierarchy itself.* One can turn the hierarchy upside down, calling good what was previously called not good and calling bad what was previously called good, and still end up with an undemocratic hierarchy.

The lauded thinkers who advanced moralistic dualism were not simply people with great ideas who, due to personal failings, just happened to accept the racist and sexist traditions of their societies. Instead, their racism and sexism were integral parts of the hierarchical ways they viewed the universe. The ideal universe, in their eyes, was not a democracy but a hierarchically structured society ruled by men like themselves. All of their ideas and thoughts were linked together and used to rationalize and support a hierarchical and undemocratic way of life.

As such, moralistic dualism is part of our honored history and traditions—and a blatant expression of an anti-democratic perspective. These traditions continue to influence us largely because we lack a critical awareness of what they are and their effects upon us and the institutions that are a part of our culture.

Accordingly, it should not surprise us that getting rid of moralistic dualism in favor of democratic values will be a long-term, difficult task. It should also not surprise us that a consequence of this honored history is that "democracies" like the United States are still dominated by men from upper-class backgrounds, in spite of recent progress in increasing diversity in leadership positions. Still deep in our unconsciousness is the belief that men, especially men of wealth, are more likely than others to be rational and better suited to lead and rule. This is how things will remain until the values of democracy become stronger and more widespread than they are today.

But we totally miss the point if we blame these lauded thinkers of the past for our misdeeds of the present. We are responsible for accepting the anti-democratic views of these men or moving on instead to the furthering of democracy. Our traditions do not determine the future. We do. We can stop being enemies of democratic values by understanding better what these values are and separating them from moralistic dualism.

Why Moralistic Dualism Is Inherently Unreasonable

Since moralistic dualism provides a justification for elitism, racism and sexism, it can be sensibly rejected because of its unacceptable social consequences. But it can also be rejected as inherently unreasonable.

In the case of each of these famous men, they advanced a point of view that defined and justified an elite of which they themselves were members. They defined the people who are the most good, whether in terms of reason or faith, as an elite like themselves. Each of them argued that the good should control the not-good, so accordingly the elite of which they were a part should control those not in the elite. Since only the elite know what is good, those who disagree with the elite must therefore lack understanding of what is good. Those who lack this understanding cannot be a part of the elite. Instead, they should be controlled by those who have this understanding. Thus, the elite should disregard and even suppress the views of those who do not agree with them, for those views do not come from the proper source.

The result of this way of thinking is a closed system that insulates the elite from criticism.

Once a person is safely inside such a closed system, there is no way out. If I believe myself to be superior and therefore a member of the true elite, then anyone who thinks otherwise must be inferior and outside the true elite. If I think of myself as rational, then anyone who thinks I am not must be irrational. If I think of myself as a true believer, then anyone who questions my faith must be an unbeliever. In this way I reject the only way out of the circle, which would be to accept as my equal those who differ from me. Instead, I designate them as inferior and preserve my self-anointed superiority. Systems that are fully enclosed in circular thinking are inherently irrational.

Consider, for example, someone who says that being a Christian is essential to being good. Therefore, anyone who is not a Christian is not good. There is no reason even to listen to a non-Christian. In the case of Luther and Calvin, the non-Christians should even be oppressed and killed.

Or consider Freud's view that Europeans are superior to non-Europeans. Given this belief, there is no reason why he would listen to the views of a non-European. If even another European questioned the superiority of Europeans, it would be a sign that he does not understand the need for instinctual renunciation. Those who do not understand this need are necessarily deficient and should be controlled by the elite. Those who do not understand this need can, thus, not only be disregarded but also made subject to the elite's authority.

For all these famous men, women are automatically excluded from the elite (although Plato allowed for exceptions to the general rule). It follows that nothing a woman says needs to be given serious consideration simply because she is not a man. Only those defined as part of the elite are qualified to say anything worthy of serious consideration, and women are automatically excluded.

The continuing relevance of this old and continuing tradition of male supremacy is that most women today, in spite of much progress, have encountered men who do not take them seriously and who attribute their views to their inherent emotionality, irrationality, or hysteria. On occasion these men are (at least for a while) their own husbands. These contemporary men, like their ancient and modern predecessors, are locked in their own circle of irrationality that prevents them from seriously considering any way of thinking but their own. Fortunately the numbers of men like this appear to be diminishing.

In short, moralistic dualism is a closed system of self-affirming assertions that are immune to questioning. It is a system based on irrational circular reasoning: "Good is what I say it is and if you disagree, you are not good and therefore I do not have to listen to you." Furthermore, those who are good are the elite who should control those who are not the elite, and any protest against that control by those not a part of the elite should be ignored or stifled. This circular way of thinking is a core ingredient of anti-democratic mentality.

The assertion of human equality in the Declaration of Independence was much more than a rallying cry against British rule. It was a revolutionary assertion of a new way of thinking and living that countered many centuries of the elitist tradition. By asserting human equality and the right of the people to select their own representatives to govern, the writers of the Declaration were saying (more than they themselves realized at the time) that members of an elite do not have preference in deciding how we are to be governed. Yet, these same writers were themselves elitists who could only partially wrest themselves away from the anti-democratic mentality with which they were imbued. Their own failings, and those of subsequent generations including our own, have prevented the values of democracy from being fully implemented. But at least we understand today that democracy means "one person, one vote" in choosing how we are governed; that the vote should extend to everyone, not just to an elite; and that no individuals should be presumed superior or better qualified to choose their representatives than others.

The assertion of human equality avoids the fatal flaw of moralistic dualism by saying that the views and opinions of anyone may be wrong. Furthermore, no group, however defined, has any special right or privilege to select rulers from among themselves or to suppress the views of those who disagree with them. This breaks open the closed circle of reasoning that preserves elitism and instead allows differing points of view to be subject to debate and criticism, regardless of who holds the view or who questions it.

It also means that those who voice opposition to democratic values are equal to those who support these values. Their views too must be allowed to be openly expressed and critiqued in the light of day.

Why Believing in Evil Attracts Us

We are all tempted to believe that wrongdoing in the world is caused by others and that we are on the side of goodness. Every governmental leader in the world gains popular support by proclaiming that wrongdoers exist elsewhere and that we, the good people, must fight against them. We are comforted by such thoughts and send our sons and daughters off to war to sustain our comfort.

Such beliefs allow moralistic dualism to govern us: We are good. They are bad or evil. Therefore, anything they say or do is bad or evil. We cannot negotiate or engage in mediation with them, for that means compromising with evil. They must be defeated. Since we are good and they are evil, we can feel good about ourselves if we kill them.

To maintain this view, we have to dehumanize these "bad" others by removing from them essential human traits. One essential human trait is the ability to change, to exercise free will, to admit one's mistake and correct it going forward. We can remove this human trait by calling the wrongdoer "evil." An evil person cannot change. They are permanently infected by a mythical evil. Thus, they will always be evil. They have no free will. By calling them "evil," we have removed their humanity from them and can then, in good conscience, attack and kill them. This concept is an essential tool in the hands of political and religious leaders who wish, for whatever reasons, to declare war on others or to conquer or control them.

But just as moralistic dualism is an irrational model of circular reasoning, so too is the idea that we can identify others who are evil. Such identification prevents us from listening to their side of the story: You don't listen to evil; you don't negotiate with evil. But by calling "evil" those who oppose us and by refusing to listen to them, we remain blind

not only to their points of view but also to our own misdeeds
to which they may alert us.

But Some People Do Awful Things

Defenders of moralistic dualism will point to the fact that
some people do terrible things. They are certainly correct.

But it is one thing to see horrible, horrendous acts and
even to call them evil deeds. It is another thing to say that the
people who committed those acts are evil. It does not logically
follow that the one who commits an evil deed is an evil
person. Yet, we lump the two together—the deed and the
person—as though they were one. But distinguishing the deed
from the person who commits the deed is critical to
understanding how democratic values differ from moralistic
dualism.

To say that a person is evil is to suggest that the person is
inhabited by an unchangeable force that can never be good. It
is to say that the person has no free will but is instead
controlled by this evil force. It is to deny that person's
humanity, to indict his soul. No good can come from such a
person.

But how can we know that anyone is really evil? How do
we know that it is not those who call others "evil" who are
evil? In other words, if we believe evil people exist, how do
we know that we are not the evil ones? An evil person would
surely be thoroughly engaged in self-deception and accuse
others of being evil. As is common in war, each side thinks the
other is evil. How are we to know that the other side is not
right? What makes us the good people other than our own
capacity for self-deception and illusion—and the circular
belief that since we are good, it must not be us who are evil?
If we are evil, we would surely use self-deception and circular

thinking to convince ourselves that we are good, not evil.

Once we question our capacity to know who is evil and who is not, we can begin to look at matters differently. Since democratic values respect the equal worth of others, the goal in a democracy is to minimize the harm anyone does to anyone else. The harm to be minimized may be one individual hurting another; it may be social systems causing some to suffer while others benefit from the suffering. In any event, harm to others is something that can be observed and measured, sometimes easily, sometimes with great difficulty. These are things that are subject to factual studies and scientific inquiry. Such studies and inquiry require no metaphysical assumption about "evil."

Thus, it is one thing to see terrible things and determine who committed them. Those deeds and their perpetrators are visible or can be found. Witnesses can describe what they saw. Perpetrators can be identified based on what people have seen. Suspects can be captured and brought to trial. Laws can be applied to the facts to determine what should happen to those apprehended and to decide whether they should be confined or set free.

But it is another thing to say that the terrible thing that happened was caused by an evil person or evil people. If we say a person did a terrible thing because he is evil, we are making a metaphysical inference about something invisible. No one ever sees evil. Unlike a virus, evil has never been seen under a microscope. There is no evil gene. Believing someone is evil is an inference. The inference is possible only if we believe that people can be infected by this invisible thing called "evil" that makes them unable to be anything other than evil. The existence of such an "evil" is nothing more than a conjecture that cannot be proven. Such conjectures should have no place in governing how we treat others or in determining social and political policy.

How Do We Protect Ourselves From Awful Deeds?

So what do we do with people who do awful things? If they are not evil, how do we justify capturing them, bringing them to trial and imprisoning them?

The justification comes from the need to protect ourselves and others from harm. If someone intentionally injures or kills another, we need to protect ourselves and others from the likelihood that the wrongdoer will do it again. If the wrongdoer is put in prison or otherwise confined, we have succeeded in preventing him or her from doing further harm. We do not need to assume that the wrongdoer is evil or a bad person. We only need to know that the wrongdoer has unjustifiably harmed another and may do so again.

Imprisonment of wrongdoers, thus, is justified as a means of preventing the wrongdoers from doing more harm. But since the wrongdoers are also human beings whose lives are of equal worth to our own, we cannot kill the wrongdoers. We should not even mistreat the wrongdoers beyond what is necessary to protect ourselves and others from the wrongdoers' repeating the harms they have already done. If later we become convinced that the wrongdoers are not going to do more harm, they should be released and given assistance to reenter society as contributing members.

A further reason for imprisoning the wrongdoers is to require them to engage in activities that aid the victims or the survivors of the victims. Doing this would hold them responsible for their harmful acts in a constructive way. Compensating victims of crime is something that is very poorly done in the United States. Victims of crime are often inadequately compensated if at all. One way to compensate victims is to engage wrongdoers in labor that produces income that is put into a fund to aid the victims.

When instead we treat the wrongdoers as evil people and abuse them or kill them, or deny them due process, we act as the enemy of democratic values. When we intentionally injure the wrongdoer beyond confinement, we go beyond what is necessary to protect ourselves and the continued functioning of society. In short, by intentionally abusing wrongdoers beyond what is necessary to protect ourselves, we become wrongdoers ourselves and engage in the very "evil" we are combating. At the same time, by ignoring the welfare of the victims, we thoughtlessly ratify what the wrongdoers have done by leaving the harmed victims to fend for themselves.

Why We Must Overcome the Idea of "Evil"

The idea that there is a force of evil that is identifiable by us, that infects people and makes them evil, is an idea that has no place in a democratic society.

The idea is useful in undemocratic societies. Maintaining a hierarchical social order requires instilling fear in the populace so they do not rebel. Proclaiming that we are threatened by some unseen evil is an effective way for those in power to keep us fearful and willing to submit to higher authority out of fear that we will either be attacked by evil or accused of being evil. When the sovereign power wants war, "evil" can always be called upon to rally the populace against those to be attacked. The fight against evil is intrinsically a noble thing.

Unfortunately, the same idea of evil that was integral to our ancestors' undemocratic past continues to survive. This idea has been brought forth during some of the most undemocratic moments in the history of the United States. During the Cold War the evil target consisted of "communists." In certain parts of the United States for most of its history, and even today in certain places, the evil ones included blacks, Native Americans, and homosexuals. In the Declaration of Independence, the evil ones were designated as the "merciless Indian savages." Today the evil ones are whomever we designate as "terrorists" and "suspected terrorists." It is this way of thinking that legitimizes oppression, torture, war and genocide and even makes it seem honorable. That the fight against evil is noble and honorable is an idea that every government relies on to kill and oppress but is based on conjecture, self-deception and illusion.

Designating others as "evil" is both arrogant and ignorant. Who are we to believe that we have the power and insight to know who is and who is not evil? What makes us superior to the others we call evil who may themselves believe that we, not them, are the evil ones? Believing that there is a force of evil that invades the souls of others (not ourselves, of course) falsely assumes that we are imbued with superior knowledge or insight that enables us to correctly know who is and is not evil. Once we falsely assume that righteous perspective, we close ourselves to the possibility that we may be wrong.

The idea that certain others are evil is appealing, because it comforts us to believe that we are good and superior. That belief is an illusion. It is a variation of the idea that God is on our side and, by implication, not on the side of anyone who does not like us or agree with us. This belief is used to justify the oppression of others and deny due process to whomever the government wants to call a "suspected terrorist" or some other bad name it decides to use. We can—and do—imprison and kill people as long as we sincerely believe they are "suspected terrorists," people suspected of being evil.

This same mentality in the late Middle Ages led to the torturing and killing of women designated as witches. Similarly, women designated as witches were hanged in the American colonies. This same mentality today creates new witches using different names.

Instead of using conjecture to designate some as evil, we need instead to abandon conjecture and make judgments based on facts, common sense and open-minded, reasoned inquiry. Resolving social and international conflict requires careful analysis and scientific inquiry into the complexities of cause and effect. The conjecture of evil gets in the way. Instead of leading us to open-minded inquiry, it requires us to look for "evil" people to capture, confine or kill. Determining who is "evil" is not a matter of open-ended inquiry but is based on prejudice and unexamined beliefs. It also rejects the principle of democracy that all people are of equal worth.

Why are democratic values preferable to the idea that some people are evil? Because believing in democratic values requires us to recognize that we cannot presume to have the perspective of God and determine who is evil. It requires us to respect the inherent worthiness of every human life, whether or not we think that a particular human life has gone badly astray. It also requires us to recognize our own worth and protect ourselves, but only by doing the minimum necessary to prevent others from harming us and others, without crossing the line to become abusers, aggressors and oppressors.

Democratic values mean that all people are of equal worth. No one is so worthless as to deserve to die, even though at times we may unavoidably and regrettably have to use potentially lethal force to protect ourselves and others. Democratic values mean that we must listen to those who proclaim that we are their enemies and examine our own lives to see if in some way we have contributed, by action, inaction, or indifference, to the perpetuation of inhumane conditions that are the source of much of the hatred and violence that may be directed against us. Democratic values impose upon us the frightening and difficult task of considering the possibility that those who disagree with us, despise us or even attack us may have plausible reasons for doing so. Given that possibility, we should listen to them instead of conveniently designating them as our evil enemies.

In short, to accomplish what democratic values demand of us, we must eliminate the idea that some people are evil. To do so is not to abandon ethical judgments but instead to judge actions by the harm they do or the benefits they provide without allowing the idea of evil to dehumanize those we do not like. In addition, focusing on evil wrongdoers draws our attention away from potential societal structural flaws and ingrained ways of thinking that allow or cause bad outcomes within our own society.

Chapter 3

How We Advance an Anti-Democratic Mentality: Our Failure to Contest the Anti-Democratic Content of Former President George W. Bush's Global Doctrine

> *How can we avoid repeating the*
> *anti-democratic crusades of the recent past?*

Throughout the history of the United States, the public has been led into various crusades against "enemies" designated as such by the President or other governmental authorities. Some examples were campaigns to massacre or relocate Native Americans; anti-communist campaigns spanning most of the twentieth century; and the confinement and relocation of Japanese-Americans during World War II. During the presidency of George W. Bush, the enemy became "the terrorists," "suspected terrorists," and the so-called "Axis of Evil."

In each case, the "enemy" consisted of people who were not seen as equal to the rest of us, but instead were seen as evil people who must be captured, confined or destroyed. In each case, we abandoned democratic values in favor of moralistic dualism, and we did so without much subsequent awareness or regret.

These past instances of abandonment of democratic values portend the future—unless we change the way we think. In this chapter we will examine in detail the seductive, anti-democratic vision of then President George W. Bush in the hope that next time such a vision appears we will quickly see that it reflects a mentality that would lead us backwards into the undemocratic past of humankind. Because most of the public was unable to see the anti-democratic content in Mr. Bush's speeches, he was able to gather the widespread support he needed to launch an invasion of Iraq, capture and detain suspects without trial, and lead Congress to overwhelming approve measures that undermine many of the civil liberties that had developed and grown during the preceding two centuries.

Discerning the Bush Global Doctrine

Following the attacks of September 11, 2001, then President Bush began the process of convincing the public and Congress about his global vision. In the process, bit by bit, he composed and presented a doctrine—we can accurately call it his "Global Doctrine"—rooted in anti-democratic moralistic dualism.

His persuasive technique is instructive, because it was effective and will undoubtedly be used again and again. He presented his doctrine piecemeal, with each piece cloaked in disarming and seductive emotional appeals. Thus, the attractiveness of the emotional appeal covered the bit of Global Doctrine immersed within the appeal. Over time, each bit seemed acceptable, and it is only by careful analysis of his speeches that we can see that the individual pieces were part of a larger coherent picture tying together God, historical destiny, freedom, democracy, military power and the need to control the Middle East.

For example, in Bush's "State of the Union" address delivered January 28, 2003, the written text of his speech that appeared on the GOP.com website stated:

"Many challenges, abroad and at home, have arrived in a single season. In two years, America has gone from a sense of invulnerability to an awareness of peril; from bitter division in small matters to calm unity in great causes. And we go forward with confidence, because this call of history has come to the right country. Americans are a resolute people who have risen to every test of our time."

On the surface, this sounds good. "Many challenges . . . an awareness of peril . . . to calm unity . . . we go forward with confidence . . . Americans are a resolute people. . . ." How can we disagree with that?

But look again: *"This call of history has come to the right country."* "Call of history"? What is this? While it may sound like just another emotional appeal, it is one of the essential pieces of his Global Doctrine, carefully placed in the middle of a satisfying emotional appeal. Subliminally we associate this "call of history" with the emotion aroused by his seductive appeals in the surrounding text.

In another example from a speech given on May 6, 2004, at the Republican National Committee gala, again taken from the printed text as it appeared online on GOP.com:

"I've seen the unselfish courage of our troops. I've seen the heroism of Americans in the face of danger. I've seen the spirit of service and compassion that runs deep in our country. We've all seen our nation unite in common purpose when it mattered most. We will need all of these qualities for the work ahead. I am running because there's more work to do. We have a war to win. And the world is counting us to lead the cause of freedom and peace. We have a duty to spread opportunity to every part of America. We have an obligation to work together to make this country safer and stronger and better. This is the work that history has set before us. We welcome it."

Again, this sounds good. ". . . unselfish courage . . . heroism of Americans . . . spirit of service and compassion that runs deep . . . unite in common purpose . . . lead the cause of freedom and peace . . . spread opportunity . . . make this country safer and stronger and better. . . ." Fine stuff.

But look again. "We have a war to win." Which war? The war in Iraq? The war in Afghanistan? The war "against terror"? Are there three wars or just one? Are they all the same? What does it mean to win a war that has been unilaterally announced and unilaterally begun with invasions? Is it true that "the world" is counting on us to lead the cause of freedom and peace? If so, then why are we at war with a significant part of the world? Why is winning a war related to the cause of peace and freedom? And what is this work that "history" has set before us? Again, what is this "history" that somehow acts as an authority over national policy?

These questions do not arise when the controversial phrases are successfully cloaked in uncontroversial emotional appeals. The result is subliminal persuasion. While this persuasive technique is a legitimate and frequently used rhetorical device, it shifts the burden to the listener to filter out emotional appeals from cold content. Such calmness was mostly absent when the nation was in a state of fear about "terrorism" and the "terrorists" who must be lurking among us.

Mr. Bush's defenders may protest that the Global Doctrine that emerges when the rhetoric is stripped away is the product of quoting out of context. But when the surrounding context consists of rhetorical techniques designed to persuade, eliminating this emotion-laden context is the only way to find the core message.

If President Bush had named and presented his Global Doctrine directly, stripped of the agreeable emotional appeals, he would have made the following speech.

(The italicized text—the brief introduction, conclusion, and the headings of each point—is mine. The rest consists of direct quotes taken from a wide sampling of Mr. Bush's written speeches, proclamations, and recorded remarks at press conferences and other occasions that appeared on the websites GOP.com or whitehouse.gov from 2001 through 2007. The number after each quote references the particular speech from which the quote came. These speeches and their corresponding numbers are listed in note fifty-five [55] in the Notes at the end of the book. Many other speeches, proclamations and remarks not quoted here contained similar messages.)

≈≈≈

THE TEN POINTS OF FORMER PRESIDENT GEORGE W. BUSH'S GLOBAL DOCTRINE

(Applause.) Thank you. Good evening. Tonight I will present and explain to you the ten points of my Global Doctrine, a doctrine to

lead our great nation and the world to peace and prosperity in the challenging and difficult years ahead.

POINT 1 (BUSH): THE UNITED STATES IS A GREAT AND PEACEFUL NATION.

"We're a great nation" (4). "We're a peaceful nation" (8). "We have a great country. We're a great people" (13). "We go forward . . . confident in the future of the greatest nation on earth" (27). "We go forward to defend freedom and all that is good and just in our world" (1). "This great nation . . . will defend freedom" (6).

POINT 2 (BUSH): OUR CAUSE IS RIGHT, NOBLE, AND BLESSED BY GOD.

"Our cause is just, and it continues" (16). "We are engaged in a noble cause. . . " (6). "Overcoming evil is the noblest cause. . . . We are applying the power of our country . . . to serve the cause of justice" (22). "We must also remember our calling as a blessed country is to make this world better" (20). "We all know that this is one nation, under God" (10). "I believe there's an Almighty, and I believe the Almighty's great gift to each man and woman in this world is the desire to be free" (35). "Freedom and fear, justice and cruelty, have always been at war, and we know that God is not neutral between them" (3). "We can trust in that greater power Who guides the unfolding of the years. And in all that is to come, we can know that His purposes are just and true. . ." (25). "Freedom is not America's gift to the world, it is the Almighty God's gift to every man and woman in this world" (27). "I believe that God has planted in every heart the desire to live in freedom. . . . So America is pursuing a forward strategy of freedom. . ." (25). "As we have been assured, neither death nor life, nor angels nor principalities nor powers, nor things present nor things to come, nor height nor depth, can separate us from God's love. . . . May He always guide our country" (2). "We acknowledge, especially now, our dependence on One greater than ourselves. . . . Almighty God . . . is our refuge and our strength in this time of trouble . . ." (14).

POINT 3 (BUSH): WE ARE WITHOUT FAULT IN THE PRESENT CONFLICT.

"The United States and other nations did nothing to deserve or invite this threat" (21). "How do I respond when I see that in some Islamic countries there is vitriolic hatred for America? I'll tell you how I respond: I'm amazed. I'm amazed that there is such misunderstanding of what our country is about, that people could hate us. . . . Because I know how good we are. . . . We're fighting evil" (9). "Why do they hate us? . . .They hate our freedoms" (3).

POINT 4 (BUSH): THE UNITED STATES' SPECIAL CALLING AND HISTORICAL MISSION IS TO SPREAD PEACE, DEMOCRACY AND FREEDOM AROUND THE WORLD, AND TO SAVE CIVILIZATION AND THE WORLD.

"Freedom is the birthright and deep desire of every human soul, and spreading freedom's blessings is the calling of our time" (29). "We have a calling from beyond the stars to stand for freedom" (27). "We're determined and resolute to answer the call to history. . . " (17). "We will meet the responsibility that history has given us" (42). "The advance of human freedom—the great achievement of our time, and the great hope of every time—now depends on us" (3). "Our Nation is committed to an historic, long-term goal—we seek the end of tyranny in our world" (36). "History has called America and our allies to action, and it is both our responsibility and our privilege to fight freedom's fight" (22). "The world is counting on us to lead the cause of freedom and peace. . . . This is the work that history has set before us" (26). "It is a war to save the world" (6). "It is a struggle for civilization" (37). "This is not, however, just America's fight. . . . This is the world's fight. This is civilization's fight" (3). "We wage a war to save civilization, itself" (12). "This nation and all our friends are all that stand between a world at peace, and a world of chaos and constant alarm. . . . We are called to defend . . . the hopes of all mankind" (20).

POINT 5 (BUSH): THE UNITED STATES REPRESENTS AND ACTS ON BEHALF OF THE INTERESTS OF EVERYONE IN THE WORLD WHO WANTS PEACE, DEMOCRACY, FREEDOM AND LIBERTY.

"We enforce the just demands of the world. . . " (21). "America will lead by defending liberty and justice because they are right and true and unchanging for all people everywhere. . . . America will take the side of brave men and women who advocate these values around the world" (22). "We defend not only our precious freedoms, but also the freedom of people everywhere to live and raise their children free from fear " (8). "We fight for one thing, and that is the freedom of our people, and the freedom of people everywhere. . . . This nation is freedom's home, and freedom's defender" (12). "The cause we serve is right, because it is the cause of all mankind" (25). "This great nation will lead the world" (7). "We will lead the 21st century into a shining age of human liberty" (37).

POINT 6 (BUSH): THE UNITED STATES' HISTORICAL MISSION WILL BE LED BY OUR MILITARY.

"When freedom needs defending, America turns to our military" (22). "There is no higher calling than service in our Armed Forces" (31). "Our first priority is the military. The highest calling to protect the people is to strengthen our military" (15). "All in this generation of our military—have taken up the highest calling of history" (23). "Our great opportunity is to advance the cause of justice and human dignity and freedom all across the world. In this cause, our military is showing the world America at its best" (15). "In every conflict, the character of our nation has been demonstrated in the conduct of the United States military" (18). "We see America's character in our military" (27). "Wherever our military has gone, they have brought pride to our own people and hope to millions of others" (12). "Our military has brought justice to the enemy, and honor to America" (28). "In the decisions and missions to come, our military will carry the values of America and the hopes of the world" (19).

POINT 7 (BUSH): THOSE WHO OPPOSE OR THREATEN AMERICA, OR SEEK THE ABILITY TO THREATEN AMERICA, ARE EVIL, AND EVIL MUST BE DESTROYED.

"On Nine-Eleven, our Nation saw the face of evil" (37). "The people who did this act on America, and who may be planning further acts, are evil people. . . . They're flat evil" (5). "We're fighting evil" (9). "This is a war between good and evil" (6). "This great country will not let evil stand" (7). "So we're determined to fight this evil, and fight until we're rid of it" (11). "They're fighting on behalf of a hateful ideology that despises everything America stands for" (32). "The great purpose of our great land . . . is to rid this world of evil and terror" (12). "These enemies will not be stopped by negotiations, or concessions, or appeals to reason. In this war, there is only one option—and that is victory" (30).

POINT 8 (BUSH): THE UNITED STATES MUST ACT THROUGHOUT THE WORLD AND ANYWHERE IN THE WORLD TO DEFEND AMERICA AND SPREAD FREEDOM.

"Our nation is engaged in a global war on terror" (33). "It is a global effort" (41). "America is determined and resolute to not only defend our freedom, but defend freedom around the world" (19). "So we're after the enemy across the globe. And we're determined, and we're relentless, and we will stay on the hunt until the terrorists have nowhere to run and nowhere to hide" (33). "America must confront threats before they fully materialize" (26). "A threat that gathers on the other side of the earth can bring suffering to the American homeland" (18). "The only way to defend our citizens where we live is to go after the terrorists where they live" (33). "You see, this new kind of war, the first war of the 21st century, is a war on a global scale. And to protect our people, we've got to prevail in every theater" (33).

POINT 9 (BUSH): THE UNITED STATES DETERMINES WHETHER OR NOT YOU SUPPORT THE UNITED STATES, AND IF YOU DO NOT SUPPORT THE UNITED STATES, YOU SUPPORT THE TERRORISTS.

"Shortly after September the 11th, I announced a doctrine that said: either you're with the United States and those of us who love freedom or you're with the enemy" (18). "Every nation has a choice to make. In this conflict, there is no neutral ground" (8). "Either you are with us, or you are with the terrorists" (3). "America will not tolerate regimes that harbor or support terrorists" (31). "If you harbor a terrorist, if you feed a terrorist, if you provide sanctuary to a terrorist, if you fund a terrorist, you are just as guilty as the terrorist that inflicted the harm on the American people" (10). "We have developed the international financial equivalent of law enforcement's 'Most Wanted' list . . . much of which is classified, so it will not be disclosed. . . . This list is just a beginning. . . . We will freeze the assets of others as we find that they aid and abet terrorists organizations around the world" (4). "In the weeks following September the 11th, I authorized a terrorist surveillance program to detect and intercept al Qaeda communications involving someone here in the United States. This is a targeted program to intercept communications in which intelligence professionals have reason to believe that at least one person is a member or agent of al Qaeda or a related terrorist organization" (35). "Suspected terrorists have been arrested in many countries. Many others have met a different fate" (20). "No enemy that threatens our security or endangers our people will escape the patient justice and the overwhelming power of the United States of America" (18).

POINT 10 (BUSH): *BRINGING FREEDOM TO IRAQ AND THE MIDDLE EAST IS THE FIRST STEP TOWARD BRINGING FREEDOM TO THE WORLD.*

"We are in the early hours of this struggle between tyranny and freedom" (37). "We are standing with those who yearn for liberty in the Middle East. . ." (43). "Nothing is more important at this moment in our history than for America to succeed in the Middle East" (40). "The challenge playing out across the broader Middle East is more than a military conflict. It is the decisive ideological struggle of our time" (39). "The establishment of a free Iraq at the heart of the Middle East will be a crushing defeat to the forces of tyranny and terror, and a watershed event in the global democratic revolution" (29). "A stable Middle East is critical to the security of the American people" (24). "We're spreading the hope of freedom across the broader Middle East . . . . And so by advancing the cause of liberty and freedom in the Middle East, we're bringing hope to millions, and security to our own citizens" (33). "I have asked for some of your time to discuss the nature of the threat still before us . . . and the building of a more hopeful Middle East that holds the key to peace for American and the world" (37).

THIS IS MY 10-POINT GLOBAL VISION, PLAIN AND SIMPLE. I CONCLUDE BY SAYING: "From Afghanistan and Iraq to Africa and Southeast Asia, we are engaged in a struggle . . . which will help determine the destiny of the civilized world" (38). "We go forward with trust that the Author of Liberty will guide us through these trying hours" (39). "May God bless the United States of America" (25) and "continue to bless America" (5, 8, 20, 27).

≈≈≈

The Global Doctrine Summarized

When we view the Global Doctrine as a whole, we see that it says that the United States carries out God's will and the mission of history by using its military power anywhere in the world to attack any person, organization or nation that disagrees with American policy: Either you are for us or you are against us. Those who are not for us oppose freedom and are evil. Evil must be destroyed. Though the use of U.S. military power, the world will be saved, freedom will spread throughout the world, and peace will be assured.

In short, the Bush Global Doctrine is a manifesto that could be used to support an ultimate goal of United States' military control of the world, all presented benignly in the name of peace, freedom, God and democracy.

This Global Doctrine is founded in faith, not fact. Just as there was no solid evidence for "weapons of mass destruction" in Iraq when the United States invaded Iraq, there was no solid evidence that linked Iraq to the attacks of September 11, 2001. By linking 9/11 to the invasion of Iraq, and by treating all anti-U.S. violence as "terrorism" as though it was all one thing, the Bush Global Doctrine regarded the "war on terrorism" as a war against whomever the United States government alleges supports terrorism, regardless of the facts.

There can never be, of course, any facts that support the belief that the United States is on the side of God. And while we may like to believe that history inevitably advances toward democracy, that is an unprovable proposition that may well turn out to be wrong. Mr. Bush's statements in support of his Point 3 in the simulated speech that express amazement at how poor and powerless people could hate the rich and powerful United States, reveals profound historical ignorance and obliviousness to human nature. Again, facts are overwhelmed by a faith that both ignores facts and is contrary to them.

One reasonable inference from known facts should not be ignored. Wherever the U.S. invades militarily, some people will oppose it with violence. These opponents will become the new terrorists. The enemy will be created where it may not have previously existed. Thus, every U.S. invasion will create terrorism, guaranteeing a long if not never-ending war against terrorism in which victory is impossible. The United States' invasion of Iraq has already instigated the turmoil that will guarantee a long conflict, not only in Iraq but also throughout the Middle East and extending beyond it into Pakistan and possibly other nations as well.

Why the Bush Global Doctrine Undermines Democratic Values

The Bush Global Doctrine is the anti-democratic statement of an imperial power that could be used to justify the idea of controlling the world. We cannot believe that "all people are created equal" and at the same time say "you are for us or against us." We cannot believe that "all people are created equal" and divide the world into those who are good and those who are evil. We cannot believe that "all people are created equal" and assume that what we believe is right and that anyone who disagrees is wrong and may therefore be captured or killed. In short, the Bush Global Doctrine denies the values upon which democracy is founded, values which all rely on the fundamental principle, "All people are created equal." Equality is not a part of the Bush Global Doctrine.

The contradictions of the Bush Global Doctrine can be summed up in his own words: "Freedom is on the march."[56] To march is to engage in one of the least free activities of which humans are capable. To march, you must be in line and in step with everyone else. Deviation from the preset beat of the march is unacceptable. And marching is primarily a military activity—the same kind of activity that the Global Doctrine advocates.

But freedom cannot march. Freedom does not force itself on others with gunfire, tanks and bombs. Freedom means respecting diversity, accepting dissent, and encouraging the questioning of authority and accepted beliefs. This is what marching excludes.

To the extent military marching aggressively invades other lands to kill people believed to be "evil," democratic values will be trampled under the heavy feet of advancing troops.

The Continuing Influence of the Bush Global Doctrine

As President, George W. Bush gave a multitude of speeches, radio addresses and press conferences, often totaling several times per month, and also issued proclamations to persuade the American public that his Global Doctrine was right.[57] He was effective in persuading much of the public of the rightness of his ideas. His incessant rhetoric shifted the moral center of gravity away from democratic values toward acceptance of militaristic threats and conquest as the moral norm for a great power. Some of the now-common premises of his Global Doctrine—accepted by many Democrats as well as most Republicans—are that the preservation of democracy requires attacking and killing those who are considered "evil," that there is a "war against terrorism" that must be won, and that winning means a military victory.

Unfortunately, George W. Bush's dramatic departure from the path of democratic growth did not end with his term of office. His Global Doctrine is now so deeply ingrained in the American psyche that it will continue subliminally until all aspects of it are exposed and reversed. This ingrained vision resulted in changed laws that will take time and courage to rescind.

An example of these persistent changes of law occurred in 2005 when the U.S. Senate, by a vote of 49 - 42, approved a proposal to abolish the right of prisoners held in Guantanamo to challenge their detentions in federal court.[58] The same year, a similar measure limiting the right of prisoners to contest their detentions, passed by a vote of 84 - 14.[59] The pernicious Military Commissions Act of 2006 was approved by the U.S Senate by a vote of 65 - 34 and by the U.S. House of Representatives by a vote of 250 - 170.[60] The Military Commissions Act makes it possible for any legal immigrant or visitor in the United States, and apparently any U.S. citizen as well, to be designated an "enemy combatant" without evidence and detained without access to U.S. courts. In August, 2007, Congress passed and then President Bush signed into law the Protect America Act of 2007, which effectively ratified the President's previously assumed authority to spy on Americans without court oversight. In the House, 41 Democrats voted for the measure. In the Senate, 16 Democrats voted for it.[61] These are just a few examples of the depth of the changes that occurred, changes that will persist long after the invasion of Iraq.

Many of these votes were cast by Senators, both Republicans and Democrats, whose terms outlasted the Bush presidency. These votes show widespread acceptance of the view that the U.S. government has the authority to detain anyone it thinks might be a terrorist, with or without evidence, and deny them the due processes of law that U.S. citizens previously had under the U.S. Constitution. These prisoners may even be tortured and killed. This view of supreme governmental authority is one of the cornerstones of the Bush Global Doctrine—a view that is appropriate in a dictatorship, not in a democracy.

A large proportion of the general public has now become so accustomed to Mr. Bush's way of thinking that it is no longer disturbed by it. For example, when a candidate for the U.S. Senate announced that he supported water boarding—a form of torture—of captured *suspected* terrorists, and supported the denial of civilian trials to determine their guilt, there was no outrage. Instead, on January 19, 2010, the voters of the liberal state of Massachusetts elected Scott Brown to office by a wide margin over the candidate who opposed torture and supported due process for those accused of crime. This is an indication that the Bush anti-democratic mentality has become so deeply ingrained in the American psyche that most Americans now take no special notice of candidates who accept that anti-democratic way of thinking.

The Continuing Danger to Democracy

The primary danger to the continued growth of democracy

in the world is not the threats and attacks from those who oppose democracy but our own failure to affirm democratic values. The metaphysical belief that there are identifiable evil people in the world who must be captured or killed without trial, a belief explicitly conveyed by former president George W. Bush and ratified by votes of the U.S. Congress, opposes the fundamental democratic value, the belief that all people are of equal worth. The extent to which we pursue the "evil" people with the intention of killing them or detaining them indefinitely without trial is the extent to which we abandon democratic values.

The metaphysical conception that the world consists of good people versus evil people was equally shared by former president Bush and the noted leaders of the organizations that use violence to attack democratic societies, the so-called terrorists. They all share a common ground. They believe that they are good and the opponents are evil. They believe in using violence to capture or kill those designated as evil. The violence of "9/11" and the invasion of Iraq were both products of the same metaphysical way of thinking. Mr. Bush and the terrorists ride together in the same metaphysical boat, a boat in which "we" are good and "they" are evil. Continuation of this metaphysical way of thinking on a grand scale will guarantee continued warfare on a global scale. In a world full of weapons of mass destruction, the ultimate long-term outcome is predictably the destruction of human life as we know it. Such an horrendous outcome would be the result of widespread fanatical adherence to a metaphysical belief that people identified by us as "evil" must be captured or killed without regard to due process of law.

According to the simplistic good-versus-evil, you-are-for-us-or-against-us way of thinking, to suggest that those who oppose us are not evil people is at best to accept their destructive acts and at worst to support them. The challenge we face is to overcome this simplistic way of thinking and to present a well-conceived alternative that is solidly based in democratic values.

The critical task of addressing this matter lies ahead. There are no simple answers. The task will require combining our efforts with thoughtful people throughout the world who are committed not only to democratic values but also to the preservation of life on this planet.

To turn away from this task or to ignore it is to allow democratic values to deteriorate and anti-democratic ideas like those in the Bush Global Doctrine to become even more fully rooted than they are today. If instead we are passive in the face of this challenge, we ourselves also become enemies of democracy.

Chapter 4

How We Advance an Anti-Democratic Mentality: Our Acceptance of Religion in Politics and Social Policy

> *Religion has no place in governmental policy*
> *or decision-making.*

There is a critical difference between what someone believes as a matter of religious faith and the policies and laws of a society. The policies and laws of a democratic society must treat people equally regardless of their personal faiths and beliefs. But when governmental policy or governmental officials favor one religion over others—or religion over the lack of religion—the adherents of the favored religion are put into a more positive light. Whether the favoritism directly benefits members of the favored religion or simply gives them a higher and more favored profile in the public eye, the favoritism is a form of disrespect of those who have different beliefs.

Such favoritism is inconsistent with democratic values.

We have often allowed religion to intrude into governmental decision-making by our silence and lack of protest. In acquiescing to this intrusion, we help undermine a fundamental principle that sustains democracy, the separation of "church and state," of religion from government.

Former president George W. Bush exemplified what should not be done. In a written Proclamation that he issued prior to Christmas Day, 2001, he said, "Two thousand years ago, the savior of mankind came into the world." Then he proceeded to refer to the birthday of "Christ." In these statements he preached a Christian doctrine.[62] The Proclamation went on to say, "Christians believe that Jesus' birth was the incarnation of God on earth. . . . At Christmastime, Christians celebrate God's love revealed to the world through Christ. And the message of Jesus is one that all Americans can embrace this holiday season."

He repeated a similar message in a radio address on Christmas eve, 2005, again lauding the birthday of "Christ," the title given to Jesus by those who maintain he was the Son of God.[63] In another radio address, he referred to the Easter holiday, a Christian holiday, and went on to say, "Easter is the victory of light over darkness."[64]

In addition, in October, 2005, he endorsed one of his nominees for the U.S. Supreme Court, Harriet Miers, by lauding her Christian background.[65]

These are just a few examples indicating how George W. Bush used the office of President to shift the consciousness of Americans not only toward favoring Christianity over other religions, but also toward considering Christian faith as a criterion of political office.

But in a nation of many religions and nonbelievers, it is inappropriate for the President or any holder of a governmental office to favor any one of them. Throughout the growth of the United States toward increased democracy, one principle has steadily grown, and that is the separation of religion from government, of church from state.

This principle of separation, long recognized as among the keys to democracy, has not only been breached by former president Bush, it has also been breached by governmental officials and candidates for office, including both Republicans and Democrats. The major presidential candidates in the 2008 election, including the winner of that election, accepted Mr. Bush's premise of the importance of faith and sought to make it clear that they too were people of faith—Christian faith. These candidates, along with Mr. Bush, lost the awareness of the principle that government must be neutral with respect to religion and that any public profession of any particular faith by the President is in effect an endorsement of that faith in the eyes of the public. Any such endorsement works to the detriment of any other point of view, including the view that faith and belief in God are not relevant to determining who should hold governmental office and have no role in determining governmental policy.

While religion played a major role in the formation of the United States prior to, during and following the revolution of 1776,[66] the Founders of the nation who established the U.S Constitution and the Bill of Rights had the genius to rise above the prevailing religious fervor to include in the First Amendment an explicit recognition that the federal government should play no role in furthering or inhibiting religious practices.

To better understand why this principle of separation was added to the U.S. Constitution, we can learn from a bit of American history why this separation is essential to democracy.

The Instructive Views of Thomas Jefferson

Thomas Jefferson was among the prominent American leaders who stood for the proposition that the federal government must do nothing to either advance or inhibit religion. His now-famous message to the Danbury Baptist Association, states:

> Believing with you that religion is a matter which lies solely between Man & his God, that he owes account to none other for his faith or his worship, that the legitimate powers of government reach actions only, & not opinions, I contemplate with sovereign reverence that act of the whole American people which declared that *their* legislature should "make no law respecting an establishment of religion, or prohibiting the free exercise thereof" [quoted from the First Amendment of the U.S. Constitution], thus building a wall of separation between Church and State . . . .[67]

These words succinctly express the foundation for the separation of church and state and the severance of religion from government. Religion involves the relationship of the individual to his or her belief in "his God." Government has no business interfering in that relationship. Religious beliefs are not within the legitimate power of government to control. The government should be concerned with actions only, with what people do, not with what they believe—or don't believe.

Unlike former president George W. Bush, Jefferson correctly interpreted the principle underlying the First Amendment to prohibit him, as President, from making proclamations recommending religious observances.[68] While the actual wording of the First Amendment is limited to constraining Congressional law-making, Jefferson recognized that the principle underlying these words is broader: that government should not favor one religion over another, either by giving greater respect to one religion or by inhibiting the practices of another. It is this principle that protects the individual conscience, even to the point of allowing the individual conscience to believe in "his God" rather than some assumed common definition of "God." Since the way God is viewed or defined is up to the individual conscience, it is a logical extension of this principle also to protect the individual conscience of those who do not believe in God.

It is also a logical extension to apply the First Amendment principle of separation not only to the federal government but to state governments as well. At the time of the addition of the Bill of Rights to the U.S. Constitution, it was understood that the Bill of Rights—the first ten amendments—applied only to the federal government and not to state governments. Jefferson accepted that understanding and applied the principle of separation of religion from government to the federal government only. His view reflected the prevailing limited view that state governments were not bound by this principle.[69]

Yet, Jefferson's rationale extends much further than his own limited vision at the time. Logically, Jefferson's rationale applies to any government, local, state or federal. Thus, the logical consequences of Jefferson's rationale go beyond the limitations of his views at the time. As A. S. Turberville noted in another context, "Logic, if untrammelled, has a way of leading to untraditional conclusions."[70] When looking to the Founders for insight into the meaning of democracy, we must also look to the logical and reasonable consequences of their views and sort out and discard the contradictions.

In the case of separation of church and state,

"untrammelled" logic took quite a while to prevail. The extension of the First Amendment to prohibit state governments, and not just the federal government, from "respecting an establishment of religion or prohibiting the free exercise thereof" did not become clear until nearly 150 years after the ratification of the First Amendment, when in 1940 the U.S. Supreme Court, in *Cantwell v. Connecticut*,[71] held that the Fourteenth Amendment, which applies to the states, incorporates the protection of freedom of religion embodied in the First Amendment.[72] The result was that Jefferson's rationale for separating religion from government, that government should be concerned with actions and not beliefs, was logically extended to include all governments within the United States, not just the federal government. It is instructive to note that logic prevailed, but it took a long time.

Is the Separation Complete or Only One-Way?

But some religious advocates often seek to dilute the principle of separation by arguing that separation only works in one direction to prevent government from involvement in religion, but not in the other direction to prevent religion from involvement in government.[73] They argue not only that it is quite all right for religion to influence government, but even that religion *should* influence government. Thus, instead of a barrier between government and religion, there should be a one-way door that religion can push open to enter government but that cannot open from the other side to let government enter religion.

The problem with this one-way door is that once the door is open—like any door—the door is open in both directions. The purpose of government is to engage in a range of actions to benefit the public. Governmental actions, including speeches and proclamations by governmental officials, that support or express a particular religious point of view give that point of view an advantage over other points of view. The statements of former president George W. Bush, noted at the beginning of this chapter, are clear examples of that. They amount to an endorsement and advocacy of Christianity. Not even all people who consider themselves Christians would agree with all he said, so that even within Christianity his statements favor some Christian views over others. Similarly, many who believe in God do not believe in a God who supports invasion of another country and the imposition of democracy by military force (as described in the previous chapter). Mr. Bush's statements, thus, advanced a particular view of religion that many others do not hold. Stated while he was president, his views had persuasive power that strengthened his religious views at the expense of differing views. It even guided his choice of a Supreme Court Justice (though that effort failed for other reasons).

Thus, when religion passes through an open door to influence government, government becomes a sponsor of the particular religious views that have entered. That sponsorship passes back through the open door in the opposite direction and, through governmental acts, strengthens the religious views that have entered. This constitutes the "respecting an establishment of religion" that the principle of separation seeks to prevent.

This is not to say that the President or other governmental officials cannot be religious. It is instead to say that as governmental officials, they must refrain from appearing to favor any religious point of view. This includes refraining from advocacy of belief in God, for not everyone agrees about the nature of God, and skeptics should feel free to question any religious belief, including beliefs in God. To say otherwise is not to respect the individual conscience, and not respecting the individual conscience is to deny the equal worth of some based on their beliefs.

Thus, the idea of a one-way wall is chimerical. If influence is permitted in one direction, as a practical matter the influence will go back in the other direction in a way that cannot be prevented. If the separation of religion from government is to be effective, the wall separating the two must be a wall that separates in both directions. Either laws need to be passed that explicitly prohibit a governmental official from endorsing a particular religion, or the public needs to support the principle of separation of religion from government by removing from office any elected official who violates this principle or who appoints to office others who violate this principle.

The danger of breaching the wall that separates government from religion is that, over time, particular views will be considered heretical. Even now, when presidents and official slogans proclaim the United States to be a nation "under God," there is a danger that those who question belief in God, or in the particular view of God as voiced by the President, will be disrespected. This would allow a bit of the ancient concept of heresy to creep back into public favor with the force of government behind it.

The Sordid History of Heresy

A look at the history of the period called the "Middle Ages" will tell us what happens when religion controls government. Religious adherents are often adamant in asserting that their beliefs are the true beliefs and that contrary beliefs are wrong, bad and even evil. Add to this adamancy the power of government, then a religion that controls the government has the great temptation, even the duty, to use the power of government to punish those whose beliefs differ from that religion. To accomplish this, government must become primarily concerned with what people believe. It will reward those who accept the religion and punish those who do not. Thus the concept of punishing heresy is generated. Those who disagree, the "heretics," must be punished.

Clearly, those viewed as "heretics" are not equal to the believers.

These views prevailed during the Middle Ages. It is instructive for us today to know of this history.

This history was sustained by ideology based in an anti-democratic way of thinking. In the early fifth century, for example, St. Augustine considered the Church to be superior to the State and advocated that a moral State must be a Christian State. "The point he [Augustine] wants to make is that the State will not embody true justice, will not be a really moral State, unless it is a Christian State. . . . The Church is thus the only really perfect society and is definitely superior to the State. . . ."[74] In other words, Augustine advocated that the Church *should* control the State and that religion—what he considered the one true religion—*should* control government.

Under the Augustinian ideology, freedom of religion is unthinkable. There is only One Truth expressed by the Church. Those who thought differently from official doctrine were labeled "heretics." A noted modern scholar, A. S. Turberville, who wrote some of the history of those times stated:

The literal and fundamental meaning of the word

Heresy is *choosing*. The heretic is the man who selects certain doctrines, discards others, giving rein to individual preference in the realm of religious belief. Such an attitude is essentially incompatible with the conception that the truth has once and for all been delivered to the saints, that the faith is indivisible and unalterable, to be accepted in its entirety.[75]

The Augustinian conception was indeed that there was One Truth represented by the Church. "The Kingdom of God on earth was conceived, not as a vision of the future, but as a living and present reality—the Visible Church, Christendom. Church and Christendom were one, for the Church was catholic."[76]

This ideology reigned in the millennium that followed Augustine, with disastrous results. Even as late as the early seventeenth century, in the colonies, the views of a leading Puritan clergyman, John Cotton, differed only in minor ways from St. Augustine in viewing government as properly subordinate to religion.[77] Even though Cotton was no friend of Catholicism, Cotton viewed the role of the state as serving the interests of the Christian church, opposed democracy and, like many of his influential contemporaries, believed that heretics should be punished.[78]

Under these belief-control regimes, heresy was a crime. Your fate was largely determined by what you believed. Heretics did not sleep on the streets as quaint reminders to the faithful of the reason to remain faithful. Heretics were tortured and killed.

Among the many thousands of victims was the Italian philosopher, Giordano Bruno, who was burned at the stake in Rome in 1600. A noted historian of philosophy, Frederick Copleston, called Bruno "one of the leading and most influential thinkers of the Renaissance" and pointed out, "He aroused the disapproval and hostility not only of Catholic theologians but also of Calvinists and Lutherans, and his unhappy end was due . . . to his apparent denial of some central theological dogmas."[79]

In those days, the price of free thinking was often death. Bruno paid the price.

Among the victims too was Galileo, who was not killed but forced to renounce his scientific findings in favor of Church ideology.[80] In those times, religion viewed the pursuit of knowledge based on factual observations and verification of theories with hostility. The pursuit of knowledge was, in effect, a challenge to Church doctrine and, accordingly, the Church sought to suppress it. Faith was more important than knowledge. According to the faith of that time, the planets revolved in perfect circles. According to observations, they did not. If observations contradicted faith, the observations must be discarded, the views of the observer suppressed, the telescopes banned, and the observer persecuted.

Had the Church succeeded in its goal to suppress the advance of science, we would still be living today in an extension of the Middle Ages. The Declaration of Independence would never have been written, and today democracy would be seen as a heretical idea relegated to a footnote in a theological treatise.

The views of Jefferson, which reflected a later stage of the long cultural revolution that began with the Renaissance and was followed by the increasing acceptance of science and secular philosophy, were a radical departure from the millennium that followed St. Augustine. "The distinction which we of the modern world, as the Renaissance and Reformation have made it, are wont to make between Church and State, spiritual and temporal, was wholly foreign to medieval thought."[81] Had Jefferson spoken as he did a few centuries earlier, it is unlikely his words would have survived, and he would very likely have suffered the fate of Bruno.

Why Separation of Religion From Government Protects the Individual Conscience

The protection of individual conscience is a direct outcome of democratic values. Our values lie at the heart of who we are as individuals. To recognize that all people are of equal worth is to give equal respect to the values and religious beliefs of each person. No one can punish another for his or her beliefs without treating the other as less than equal. Actions may be subject to social control, but not beliefs.

But just as democratic values respect the values and religious beliefs of each individual—including the values of those who reject democracy—so do they also provide that the public domain cannot be dominated by any particular religious doctrine. Religious doctrine is based in faith and conviction. Decisions in the public domain must be based in reasoned discussion involving the free interchange of ideas. Whereas the religious faith of an individual may favor One Truth, to maintain there is only One Truth in the public domain is to advocate for the suppression of contrary views. Such suppression would violate the individual consciences of others who have different views, thereby violating democratic values.

In the Middle Ages (and still today in many parts of the world), inequality was the accepted norm. Your beliefs determined your value. If you did not believe what was acceptable to higher authorities, you could be acceptably tortured or killed. Democratic values are a complete rejection of that way of life.

The ancient idea that prevailed in the Middle Ages and is still present in some parts of the world and also exists within the United States—that religion should control government— would subordinate the individual conscience to the public realm and at the same time subordinate the public realm to the particular religious beliefs of those in power. The separation of religion and government protects the individual from governmental power just as it also protects the free interchange of ideas in the public realm.

Jefferson, along with many of his contemporaries and some of his predecessors, recognized that "religion is a matter which lies solely between Man & his God, that he owes account to none other for his faith or his worship."[82] In other words, the separation protects both the individual conscience from the public domain governed by the State, and also protects the public domain where ideas need to be exchanged and openly discussed without suppression. Our affirmation of this concept expressed by Jefferson is part of what protects us from a return to the Middle Ages.

The Public Domain: Where Facts and Reasoning, Not Faith, Should Prevail

Everything works best in its proper sphere. You would not call a brain surgeon to fix your furnace. You would not look up a psychiatrist to cater a gourmet meal. You would not call an auto mechanic to fix the roof of your house.

Similarly, religion and government have their proper spheres. Religion should not determine whether Congress votes to authorize a war or to provide funding to maintain bridges and highways. Government should not regulate our beliefs. Separating religion from government recognizes that each has its proper sphere and one should not interfere in the sphere of the other.

The proper sphere of government is the public domain. The proper sphere of religion and similar kinds of faith is the private domain. Neither should interfere with the other.

The public domain is where ideas can be freely expressed and where reasoned inquiry includes discussion among those concerned. The purpose of such free interchange of ideas and reasoned discussion is to arrive at the best solutions to public problems. As Jefferson stated decades before John Stuart Mill made it one of the cornerstones of his philosophy, "Reason and free inquiry are the only effectual agents against error."[83] Through discussion and reasoned inquiry, laws are formulated, enacted, interpreted, and revised to accommodate new circumstances and new understandings.

Laws are a part of the public domain. They affect every aspect of our public lives. They determine who gets and does not get health care and shape the health care that is provided. They determine who benefits from tax breaks and who pays a disproportionate share of the tax burden relative to their means. Laws determine our access to credit and the interest we pay for loans. They determine who gets subsidized when in trouble, who gets aid in disasters, who gets educated, and who goes off to war. They determine what means of communication are available to us, who owns the news media, and what stations can occupy particular places in the available frequency spectrum. They determine what kinds of businesses can exist and make corporations possible. They determine who gets investigated for illegal acts, who gets arrested and who goes to prison. There is little we do that is not affected by political and legal decisions that determine whether or how government will act or refrain from acting.

To be in any way rational and sensible, the making of laws must be informed by factual studies, rational analysis and careful thinking. Such studies and analysis are ways of gaining knowledge and of questioning what has previously been thought. Every conclusion is subject to further study and verification. As the process of inquiry continues and never reaches a result that is final for all time, reasonable people can have different points of view. Even the view of what is reasonable is itself subject to debate, for sometimes what appears unreasonable at first is regarded as reasonable later, and vice versa.

Democratic law cannot be based in Truth that is supposedly already known. Instead, democratic law is arrived at through democratic processes that recognize that the attainment of truth is an ongoing process that can advance but does not end. These democratic processes are established through agreements and compromise, and are designed to be both stable and subject to change. The laws that are enacted through this process, and not our privately held beliefs, properly govern those actions that affect others. Democratic processes permit debate on whether or how laws should be changed. Such debate, to be effective, must rely on observable facts in the public domain, not on privately held faiths that are immune from public scrutiny and verification.

Thus, democratic values require the separation of religion and government, both to protect individual conscience from domination by governmental authority or the public, and to prevent domination of the public by advocates of particular faiths who would, if wielding the powers of government, suppress or marginalize those who disagree or are of different faiths. To allow religious views to control government is to head back toward the horrendous days of the Middle Ages, where democracy and freedom of thought were unthinkable, where those who questioned in pursuit of the truth were branded as heretics and imprisoned, tortured and killed. To move back to those times is to repeal the Renaissance, discard all advances resulting from the scientific method, and live in a vision of the world as consisting of the people representing the Good—namely ourselves—in constant warfare with the people representing Evil, namely those who think and believe differently from us.

As we saw in Chapter 3, former president George W. Bush had a medieval vision, a vision that was in effect that of a holy war against Evil, where Evil is defined by the President of the United States, and God is narrowly portrayed as a Being who supports warfare as the proper way to advance freedom. That there was little public opposition to Mr. Bush's metaphysical vision, or even much awareness of it during his presidency, reveals how deeply ingrained this vision is in the culture and our subconsciousness. The real danger to democracy came not from former president Bush but from our silence and the widespread public acceptance of this anti-democratic vision.

Jefferson and the other Founders of modern democracy had a different vision. They recognized that the realm of conscience is private; actions are public. While conscience may lead someone to act, if those actions affect others, they are the legitimate concern of the public. It the actor wants the public to accept his or her actions that affect others, those actions must be accepted or justified in the public domain. Faith may appear to be a sufficient reason to the actor, but, since the public contains innumerable faiths, faith cannot be used to justify actions that affect others. Instead, we must appeal to public processes, including international ones, that are open to questioning, inquiry and debate.

To affirm democratic values means to respect the conscience of each individual and the faith of each individual, and it is that very respect that requires that no particular religious faith be the basis for public decisions or governmental action. This respect means, for example, that governments will not be allowed to spy on the public to find the modern-day "heretics"—those who disagree with governmental policy. Preserving this respect for individual conscience is the reason governmental action and religion must be separate and not intrude on one another.

To be not our enemy and instead to affirm democratic values, we must not respond favorably to political candidates who affirm their religious faith as a qualification for public office. What qualifies people for public office is their ability to participate in the public sphere, their ability to be open to listening, their desire to give serious consideration to opposing points of view, their ability to search for soundly based facts and act effectively on them, and their ability to participate in reasoned inquiry and discussion within an international community. Religious faith can be blind or informed. It can be held by tyrants as easily as by those who favor democracy. Thus, religious faith is not a qualification for public office. It is up to us, as members of the public, to make it clear that religious faith has no place in shaping governmental policies.

Chapter 5

What We Must Do to Implement Democratic Values

> *Here are specific steps we can take*
> *to reaffirm democratic values.*

We can stop being our enemy and actively support the values of democracy. This requires courageous effort to determine the consequences of democratic values and to implement personal, political and social change accordingly.

Democratic values have radical consequences that have not yet been fully realized. While the Founders got things started by establishing the foundations of democracy, little did they understand that "all men are created equal" meant that the people they called the "merciless Indian savages" were human beings deserving the same respect they gave themselves. Little did they realize that "all men are created equal" meant not only that slavery would have to be abolished, but also that black people must be given the same opportunities as whites, and that there can be no prohibitions against blacks integrating fully into the society. Little did they realize that "all men are created equal" could not be limited to males, that "men" must include women, that women must not be denied any of the rights and privileges accorded to men, and that married women cannot continue to be the property of their husbands. Little did they realize that their limited view of democratic values would logically lead to minimum wage laws, Social Security, Medicare and Medicaid, demands for equal educational opportunities for all regardless of gender, ethnicity, or economic and social class, and demands for universal health care.

As a society, we usually do not realize that democratic values still have not been fulfilled, and that much more needs to be done before we can legitimately claim to be living in a full democracy.

A society does not become a full democracy until it devotes every effort toward providing each of its members with the minimum resources needed to function successfully and participate in the major decisions that determine the society's direction and future. (This does not mean, however, that everyone must have an equal portion of the society's wealth. A person's intrinsic worth does not depend on that person's relative wealth.)

A look at how long it has taken to accomplish major democratic reforms is instructive. Slavery was not prohibited by the U.S. Constitution until almost 90 years after the signing of the Declaration of Independence, by the Thirteenth Amendment to the U. S. Constitution; women were guaranteed the right to vote 144 years after the signing of the Declaration, by the Nineteenth Amendment to the U.S. Constitution; taxing the right to vote was made illegal 188 years after the signing of the Declaration, by the Twenty-fourth Amendment that was reinforced a year later by the Voting Rights Act of 1965; remaining vestiges of apartheid were made illegal 188 years after the signing of the Declaration, by the Civil Rights Act of 1964 that was subsequently expanded by amendments and court decisions; laws against interracial marriages were invalidated 191 years after the signing of the Declaration, by the U.S. Supreme Court decision of *Loving v. Virginia*; and women were given a degree of authority over their own bodies with a time-limited right to have an abortion, 197 years after the signing of the Declaration, by the U. S. Supreme Court decision of *Roe v. Wade*—a decision that is still under attack and might be reversed. These are just a few highlights of the ongoing but painfully slow advance toward full democracy.

Thus, as we can see from this brief historical sketch, implementing democracy takes a long time. The task has not been completed. We are easily deluded, just as the Founders were, into believing that the present state of things represents democracy's fullest advance.

We do not have to be our enemy. We can, instead, support continued progress toward full democracy. Following are just some of the many steps that we must take:

Expand Our Understanding of the Right to Vote

We have often failed to understand that the denial of the right to vote to one is a denial of that right for all. If I vote for a candidate, and another who would have also voted for that candidate is thwarted from voting or voted but the vote was not counted for whatever reason, my vote has been nullified by the subtraction of the vote of the other. Examples of this— and the consequences—were described in Chapter 1.

The right to vote is a fundamental consequence of democratic values. Equality means nothing if it cannot be practiced so that all people can participate in the making of the decisions that affect them. Voting is one of the accepted means by which this is accomplished. Most understand this in theory, but our practice is unacceptably flawed.

We do not make it easy for people to vote. Polls are open for limited hours. In many urban areas, voting in major elections means waiting in long lines. Transportation to the polls is not uniformly provided, if provided at all. Instructions for voting are sometimes difficult to follow. Efforts to accommodate those who do not speak English are inconsistent and often missing entirely. When elections are flawed, it is very difficult to invalidate those elections and hold new ones.

As explained in Chapter 1, one of the worst of these barriers is the current use of certain kinds of electronic voting machines whose tallies cannot be verified, a relatively new and devastating assault on the right to vote. While some states have banned such machines, they are still used in some places, and there is no federal law prohibiting their use, as there should be.

Here are some remedies:

- Every voting process must have an independent way to verify the vote reliably. Many places have such a process, so obviously to do so cannot be a big problem. There is no right to vote if the vote count cannot be independently verified by reliable methods. It is that simple: No verification means that your vote can be disregarded, and no one will be able to know that it was. No reliable verification means that your right to vote has been destroyed. Your vote can disappear, and no one will ever be able to know it did. Federal law is needed to prohibit the use of voting machines that do not provide for verification, and of any machine that can be programmed to alter the actual results.

- Polls must not close until everyone in line has voted. Closing the door to the polling booths at a predesignated time when there are people still waiting to vote punishes the waiting voters for the government's inadequate provision of voting booths. If a line forms and becomes lengthy, it is the fault of the governmentally run voting process. No one should be denied the right to vote because of governmental failure to provide adequately for places to vote.

- Voting by mail must be permitted in every election to accommodate those who have difficulty getting to the polls. Free tracking of the mailed ballot and delivery confirmation should be provided. Physical frailty, illness or employer demands should not deprive anyone of the right to vote, but they do so by making it difficult to get to the polls. Voting by mail will provide an alternative. Eventually, when the process can become secure and verifiable, voting by Internet should be another alternative way of voting.

- Translation services must be readily available to assist those who do not speak English. Lack of facility with English should not deprive anyone of the right of vote.

- Those convicted of crimes must not be deprived of the right to vote. Those jurisdictions that deprive prisoners of the right to vote are reflections of how easily democratic values can be subverted by ancient ideas. "All people are created equal" does not mean that you become less than equal based on what you do, say or believe. Instead, it means that your intrinsic worth as a human being stays with you throughout your life, even if you are incarcerated. Denying prisoners the right to vote is a denial of democratic values.

- Make it a regular practice to invalidate any election where flaws in the voting process throw the outcome into question. An invalidated election would be followed by a new election. A flaw does not need to be intentional to be a flaw. The goal is to get the correct result.

These changes, to be effective, must be implemented and enforced on a federal level, not sporadically by various localities, and made applicable to all elections, local, state and federal.

In general, democratic values mean that all people must have the opportunity to participate in the decisions that affect their lives, and that no person or group should have a disproportionately greater or lesser share of the decision-making power. The outcome of an election belongs to every voter and everyone who attempted to vote in the election, not just to the candidates. Anyone who has been denied the right to vote in the election, not just a candidate, should have the right to challenge the results, whether or not the denial can be shown to have been intentional. If those challenging the election can show that enough people were denied the right to vote to throw into question the election's announced results, the election should be invalidated and held again, with the flaws corrected. The right to vote includes having the votes tabulated correctly and verified and includes voting on a ballot that is not so confusing that many mistakenly vote for the wrong candidate.

If standards like these had been implemented in the U.S. presidential elections of 2000, the voting in many parts of Florida would have been invalidated and new elections there would have been held. The deadlines that had to have been met under the laws in effect at the time would have been altered or waived to allow for new elections. In the presidential election of 2004, all elections that used unverifiable electronic machines would have been invalidated. The use of such machines is totally inconsistent with democratic values.

To support democratic values we must steer our society to implement these higher standards to protect the right to vote. Then we will take the right to vote seriously and become supporters of democracy instead of silent and indifferent contributors to the way things are now.

Support the Economic Lives and Health of All Members of Society

A democratic society must provide sufficient food, clothing, shelter, transportation and health care to enable its members to live and participate as they choose and to the extent they are able. This is what it means to value each human life equally. Resources must be available so that everyone has actual access to a nutritionally adequate diet, housing and basic health care, including preventive health care.

This means that an economic floor must be established that is high enough to allow every person who falls down to it to live a healthy and productive life. Much of the world understands this concept, but generally not in the United States, which effectively has no adequate floor and allows multitudes of homeless families to sleep unwillingly in the streets.

In the mid-1960's, the U.S. Social Security Administration developed a conservative measure of poverty that estimated the minimal income that families needed to be able to purchase food that provided the least expensive nutritionally adequate diet.[84] That measure, with subsequent revisions, has survived until today as the government's "poverty line." Those living below the poverty line cannot reasonably be expected to eat a minimally nutritious diet. Even if they were taught what such a diet consisted of, they could not afford to buy it. According to the U.S. Census Bureau, in 2006 more than one in eight Americans, 13.3 percent, lived below this poverty line.[85] Available records have not shown that the proportion of those living below the poverty line has ever dropped below 11 percent.[86]

The poverty line is not fully adjusted for the parts of the country where the cost of living is higher than average. People living at or just above the poverty line in the most expensive parts of the country are poorer, and even less able to afford a minimally adequate diet, than are people living elsewhere at the poverty line. Thus, the poverty line is a line that is too low for many people.

People with inadequate diets cannot be expected to have productive lives or to have healthy children. If people choose to eat badly when they can afford to eat well, that is their business as long as efforts are made to publicize to everyone the components of an adequate diet. But if people cannot obtain an adequate diet due to a combination of lack of income and lack of social services, that is a crime against democratic values. A society that has the capacity to fix this problem, and does not, is not a full democracy.

Just as important as an adequate diet is health care, a subject finally being addressed seriously in the United States at a national level but with virulent opposition that may yet derail the landmark Patient Protection and Affordable Care Act—enacted in 2010 and scheduled to kick in fully in 2014. The U.S. Census Bureau recorded that in 2007, an average of two out of every thirteen Americans (15.3 percent) did not have health insurance. For those without health insurance or with inadequate insurance with high deductibles, going into debt to pay for health care, particularly by paying for health care with high-interest credit cards, is a major cause of personal bankruptcies.[87] A Congressional finding in the Patient Protection and Affordable Care Act is that "62 percent of all personal bankruptcies are caused in part by medical expenses."[88] In just the first nine months of 2009 there were more than one million consumer bankruptcy filings.[89]

Most countries in the world, even relatively poor ones, have long understood the importance of health care for all. But in the United States health care for all is strongly opposed by many, and those opposed to it threaten to prevent new health care laws from taking effect. Every person who dies in the United States from lack of adequate health care may be considered a victim of the society's negligence.

Adequate health care coverage would provide people with access to preventive and non-emergency health care, including dental care, as well as with easier access to emergency health care. Preventive and non-emergency health care is essential to enabling us to function to our fullest capacities and be contributing members of our community and society. It enables us to participate in attaining "life, liberty and the pursuit of happiness." Except in situations requiring prevention of widespread infectious diseases, it is anyone's personal choice to refuse health care if offered, and no one should have health care forced upon them if they do not want it. But whenever someone who wants and needs available health care cannot obtain it, democratic values have been denied. A society that has the capacity to fix this problem, and does not, is not a full democracy.

While there are various means of fixing these problems of poverty and health care, and reasonable debates about how to best to fix them, the United States has made minimal and inconsistent progress over the past several decades. This lack of consistent progress exposes the extent to which powerful forces in the nation really do not want to fix them. These are the forces that stifle the growth of democracy. We must overcome those forces and solve these problems if we are to support democratic values and further the growth of democracy.

Here are some of the ways these problems could be fixed, although they are not the only ways:

- Increase the minimum wage or increase the Earned Income Tax Credit. The current federal minimum wage combined with the Earned Income Tax Credit is not enough for many individuals and families to live above the poverty line, even when working full-time.[90]

- Expand and adequately fund Social Security to cover all who need it to supplement their incomes so that everyone's total income is at least equal to the poverty line. At the same time, develop a poverty line that realistically assesses the income needed to eat nutritiously, taking into consideration regional and local differences in living costs.

• Provide health care for all, including dental care, without exceptions (using whatever mechanisms that can achieve this goal).

• Strengthen laws and devise new laws that protect families from evictions, including providing governmental subsidies for rental and mortgage payments to those who need it to prevent homelessness. (The effort made to do this during the 2008 – 2010 recession was quite inadequate.)

A nation that can spend hundreds of billions of dollars to invade another country to impose "democracy" by force, but cannot spend similar amounts to ensure democracy at home, has totally lost its grasp of the meaning of democratic values.

However, programs to assist those in need should be carefully designed so that they do not inadvertently or intentionally trap those in need into continuing to be needy. Programs to assist those in poverty should be geared to helping people be productive members of the society, not just sustaining them at a minimal level. What is at stake here is the recognition of the value of all human lives, which is nothing more than the implementation of democratic values. Most societies in the world do a better job of this than the United States. Even many countries that are not democracies value the lives of their citizens sufficiently to provide health care for all to the extent they are able. This is what any civilized society should do and what the United States, with our silent complicity, has historically failed to do.

Go Beyond Affirmative Action to Eliminate the Effects of Past Discrimination—and Poverty

A society that has engaged in past discrimination cannot reasonably expect that, going forward, treating everyone the same will result in equality, even if that change could suddenly be made. Thinking that treating everyone the same will solve the problem of discrimination simply ignores the impact of the past and blindly pretends the past never existed. Eliminating discrimination is not enough.

As an illustration: If you favor one young tree over another for ten years, giving it sufficient water and nutrients and allowing it to grow with sufficient sunlight while depriving the other tree of the same age and keeping it in shade, the favored tree will thrive while the other becomes stunted. If you then decide to treat the two trees the same after ten years of unequal treatment, the stunted tree may begin to continue to grow as rapidly as the favored tree, but will never catch up. To expect it to catch up is unrealistic. After twenty years, a newcomer looking at the two trees who did not know of the treatment of the first ten years, and seeing that they are being treated the same, would decide that the favored tree was somehow a better specimen and perhaps begin to look for genetic differences as an explanation. What the newcomer lacks is knowledge of the trees' history.

Similarly, we cannot expect that people who have been discriminated against for decades or centuries—including women, blacks, nonwhite Hispanics, Native Americans, and whites living in areas that have been impoverished for long periods—can somehow erase the effects of history even if they are suddenly treated the same as middle-class and upper-class whites. Equal treatment, even assuming it could be actually attained, would only perpetuate the effects of past discrimination, allowing those formerly discriminated against to grow as fast but never catch up.

Affirmative action—various programs that give some form of special recognition or preference to those identified as victims of past discrimination—can be valid attempts to counter the effects of past discrimination. But currently these programs are inadequate and, in many instances, unfair.

They are inadequate, because they are mostly targeted at adults after they have been damaged by past discrimination. To give the stunted tree extra nutrition after ten years of deprivation may help the stunted tree to catch up, but it will take many years. The affirmative effort should be made nonetheless, even though it will not accomplish immediate equality. It is better to make this effort than to do nothing to help remedy the bad treatment of the past. To this extent, affirmative action programs can be designed to be sound social policy.

However, some of these programs are unfair. For example, the growth of the two trees could be equalized more quickly by depriving the favored tree as well as providing extra nutrition to the stunted tree until they are equal. But this would not be fair to the favored tree. Why should the favored tree be treated poorly to correct past inequities that the favored tree benefited from but did not cause? Affirmative action programs that set and rigidly adhere to quotas effectively deprive the favored tree by putting a ceiling on how much it can grow. To the extent programs set ceilings to stifle or prevent achievements beyond the ceiling is the extent they are not sound social policy.

In addition, affirmative action programs that do not distinguish between those growing up in poorer communities and those growing up in middle class communities are overly focused on ethnicity and gender. Those who are most disadvantaged live in poorer communities, and many of them are "white," disadvantaged by long-term poverty and its consequences. Thus, affirmative action has been overly focused on ethnicity and not enough on all of the factors that have put various groups at a disadvantage—including the effects of racism and gender discrimination.

More importantly, the debate over affirmative action programs misses a bigger problem that can be addressed only for people of very young ages. People are disadvantaged by poverty and below-average income. One of the biggest impacts of this poverty is the perpetuation of below-average educational levels. School districts with low-performing schools, on average, are districts with below-average income and where parents have below-average education. Children who grow up in these school districts are at a disadvantage. These disadvantaged districts can be identified by a combination of income and the educational levels of those living there. Children growing up in these districts will generally not get the education needed to compete equally with those growing up in average and above-average districts.

There will always be individuals who defy the averages and excel regardless of their background, but if we are serious about providing quality education to those in educationally disadvantaged school districts, we will not allow those individual achievers to be convenient excuses for neglecting the relatively impoverished environment from which many of them came. Thus, for example, the election of President Obama is irrelevant to the general problem of past discrimination against African-Americans.

Correcting the educational imbalance in school districts would get closer to the root of the problem of discrimination and make a major contribution toward remedying it. First, there is an economic imbalance that is largely caused by taxation policies that tie the funds for schools to the property taxes of the schools' local districts. Poorer communities will generate less tax revenue for their schools. It is a self-perpetuating system that will not bring quality education to poorer communities. Even statewide funding of schools will not solve the problem, because some states are much poorer than others. A national system of school financing is needed to provide extra funding to poorer areas of the country and to provide incentives to attract good teachers to those areas. What is needed is *additional* funding to support poorer areas, not a diversion of funds from one place to another.

Correcting the economic imbalance of school districts would be a major and essential step forward in correcting the inequality of education that exists throughout the United States. However, more will be needed. Extra incentives will be needed to draw good teachers to school districts with a background of poverty. These two steps—(1) correcting the economic imbalance among school districts, and (2) providing incentives to attract good teachers to school districts in poorer communities—would accomplish much more than those affirmative action programs that have a positive impact on adults but little impact on the education of children. This is not to say that these approaches should replace affirmative action programs, but that they supplement the affirmative action programs that do not rely on quotas or place ceilings on any group's opportunities.

Some may object to this approach in the belief that focusing on poverty does not address the discrimination against women and ethnic minorities that has nothing to do with economic class. There is a lot of truth to this that must be acknowledged. For example, if there is a persistent cultural bias against teaching female children mathematics and science in the same way that male children are taught, this bias may have nothing to do with economic class. However, school districts that are adequately financed at least have the resources to provide additional math and science education to women and to the males and females of any ethnic minority with lower than average test scores in these subjects. Poorer school districts will not have the resources to address this problem. Thus, while equalizing the financing of school districts across the nation does not directly address the effects of discrimination based on ethnicity and gender, it would at least provide the poorer school districts with greater ability to provide extra resources to make it possible to solve the problem.

In addition, the effects of past discrimination are primarily economic. Those discriminated against earn less and, on average, live in poorer communities. Thus, addressing the most serious effects of poverty will assist those most affected by discrimination. It will also address the effects of poverty on economically disadvantaged whites—a problem that has long been neglected. In addition, by focusing on correcting these effects of discrimination, it will address the problems of those most in need. Middle-class ethnic minorities living in middle class communities generally do not need affirmative action programs or economic assistance. Instead, they need existing laws against discrimination to be vigorously enforced.

Equalizing funding of schools throughout the nation may seem like a radical proposal to some. It certainly would require a radical change from the present system of funding schools. In the present world, democratic values are still radical values, even in so-called democracies. Most who profess democratic values do not fully understand their consequences. A society which throughout its history has failed to correct the economic imbalance in its school districts can hardly be said to have achieved what democratic values require. Unless the imbalance is corrected by bringing up the economic bottom while avoiding putting ceilings at the top, the effects of past discrimination will never be overcome. To fail to correct this imbalance is to deny democratic values.

Expand the Protection of Free Speech Beyond its Current Boundaries

Free speech is part of the essential foundation of any democracy. In the United States, free speech is protected by the free speech clause of the First Amendment to the U.S. Constitution. It states, "Congress shall make no law . . . abridging the freedom of speech, or of the press . . . ." This is now generally interpreted to mean that no governmental body may restrict speech based on its content or punish speakers based on what they say or write. There is an exception for speech that is believed to cause injury directly, such as pornography or libel, and such speech may be restricted, penalized, or give rise to a civil claim for payment of damages.

But the free speech clause has a critical limitation. This limitation is that it protects speech against governmental action but not against powerful nongovernmental entities, such as corporate employers, religious institutions, and news media. The core purpose of the free speech clause, but not its only purpose, is, as Alexander Meiklejohn stated, to protect "the freedom of those activities of thought and communication by which we 'govern.'"[91] However, nongovernmental entities can destroy that freedom as effectively as an unfettered government.

For example, in 2005 Jamie Reidy authored and published a book, *Hard Sell: The Evolution of a Viagra Salesman*, that contained criticism of certain practices of the pharmaceutical industry. His employer, Eli Lilly & Co., a major pharmaceutical company, fired Reidy explicitly for what he said in the book.[92] Since the First Amendment does not restrict the activities of nongovernmental bodies, Reidy's firing was not a violation of the First Amendment or any other law. If a governmental agency had done the same thing in this kind of situation, it would have been a violation of the First Amendment.

This example illustrates the point that the First Amendment does not prevent corporate employers from firing whomever they like for what they say. The idea that the First Amendment adequately protects freedom of speech is unsound. It only protects freedom of speech against governmental interference. In any locality that is dominated by a few large corporate employers, the employers often can, without violating any law, have significant control over the political expression in that locality by making it clear to their employees that saying certain things or openly supporting a particular candidate for office will get them fired. Such activities suppress free speech and effectively undermine "the freedom of those activities of thought and communication by which we 'govern.'"

Thus, a major task ahead of us is to establish democratic values in the private sector. The principle of the First Amendment, an essential part of democratic values, needs to be spread to protect everyone from the actions of nongovernmental entities that inhibit the kind of speech that is currently protected by the First Amendment against governmental interference.

The First Amendment does not prevent Congress from enacting laws that prevent private employers from abridging the freedom of speech of employees. We can anticipate many years if not many decades of struggle to get such laws passed, just as it took many decades of struggle, starting with early efforts to end slavery, before Congress passed extensive civil rights laws in the 1960's protecting the employment, voting rights, and fair treatment of ethnic minorities and women. To fulfill democratic values, we must expand the protection of freedom of speech to protect the speech of employees against their private employers comparable to the protection citizens have against the government.

Use Internet Technology to Greatly Broaden the Base of Financial Support for Political Candidates

Politicians are beholden to their contributors. Most politicians receive most of their contributions, directly or indirectly, from wealthy individuals and large corporations. For this reason, a very small percentage of the population has a much greater influence on political decision-making than the rest of the public. There is nothing democratic about this.

The solution is to get the general public directly involved in providing the primary financial support for political candidates.

The solution is not to limit what others contribute, because such efforts have proven to have failed. They have failed not only because of court opinions, but also because they are conceptually flawed. The conceptual flaw is the belief that contributing to candidates can be meaningfully separated from contributing to the advancement of views on political issues. For these limits to succeed, such separation would have to be feasible. But while it is possible for laws to limit contributions to a political candidate, it is not possible for laws to limit contributions made to advance a point of view on a political issue, for that is a matter of free speech that cannot be constrained by governmental action. It would be contrary to free speech to make it illegal to spend more than a preset amount of money on advertisements to promote a point of view.

To treat spending on a candidate as separate from spending to advocate a point of view is not realistic. If the advertised point of view happens to be openly agreed with by a political candidate, nothing can prevent anyone who has seen the political advertisement from connecting the advertised point of view to the candidate. Thus, all the money spent on the advertisement indirectly supports the candidate who openly agrees with the advertisement, and the money spent on the advertisement cannot be limited.

Thus, it would be a violation of free speech for the government to limit the number of advertisements a person can purchase to promote a point of view. It would also be a violation of free speech and freedom of association for the government to prevent anyone from contributing to a group that wants to advance a particular point of view. For example, if you want to support a group that advocates (or opposes) permitting same-gender couples to marry, the government cannot limit your contributions to that group, for it is your right to associate with the group that advances a political point of view that you want to support. That group, in turn, cannot be prevented or limited by the government in the amount of political advertising it wants to pay for.

But if candidate A supports same-gender marriage and opposing candidate B is against it, any advertisement for permitting same-gender marriage is in effect an advertisement that gives support to candidate A. So limiting the amount of money that can be contributed directly to Candidate A is circumvented by contributing to the support of the views that A agrees with. There is no way to prevent this consistent with the First Amendment.

Thus, limiting the amount of money a candidate can spend, or limiting the amount of money that can be contributed to a political candidate, is futile, for the amount of money that can be spent to promote a point of view that a candidate may agree with cannot be limited without suppression of free speech or freedom of association. The voter will generally connect the point of view to the candidate, so that promotion of a point of view that a candidate promotes becomes in effect a promotion of the candidate.

The problem of wealthy people and corporations controlling candidates through campaign contributions and financial support of political points of view can be solved only when a large proportion of the public contributes enough to make the additional money contributed by the wealthy less of a factor. The only way to counteract big contributions from a few wealthy sources is with small contributions from millions of ordinary people.

For example, say hypothetically that for a particular campaign it takes a floor of $200 million to run the campaign effectively. If all of that $200 million comes from a large number of small contributions from a broad spectrum of the public, then an additional $200 million contributed by the wealthy will be of less significance to the candidate, because if the candidate loses the $200 million from the wealthy, the candidate will still have the $200 million floor, obtained from the broader public, that is needed to run an effective campaign. But if, instead, nearly all of the $200 million floor comes from the wealthy and the wider public contributes very little, then the candidate must serve the interests of the wealthy contributors if the candidate wants to be re-elected, for that $200 million floor is the least amount of money (in this example) that is essential to running an effective campaign.

Providing that floor with small contributions from the general public is the minimum goal to be achieved to diminish the influence of the wealthy. The more that additional funds above the floor are provided by the general public, the less the candidate has to consider the wishes of the wealthy contributors.

Thus, energy that is focused on the 2010 decision of the U.S. Supreme Court that removed restrictions on corporate financing of elections may be misdirected.[93] The energy to change campaign financing should primarily be directed toward getting the general public involved in adequately financing elections through millions of small contributions.

The problem of getting a sufficient number of small contributions to offset the influence of the wealthy is already being partially solved through the use of the Internet. Former presidential hopeful Howard Dean in 2003 and 2004 had no problem raising all the money he needed from small contributions from approximately a quarter of a million people, using the tool of the Internet. President Barack Obama, when running for President in 2008, similarly raised enormous sums from small donations from millions of ordinary people who contributed "online."[94] As the proportion of the population that uses the Internet increases, the Internet can provide the solution for candidates who do not want to be beholden to huge contributions from a small number of wealthy sources. The Internet can easily enable millions of people to contribute small amounts, thus generating as much money as needed to run an effective campaign. However, this works only if we make these contributions.

The candidate who relies on such contributions will be beholden to a wide spectrum of the populace and not, as elected officials have mostly been, primarily to the wealthy.

In the 2008 presidential election, President Obama probably had the broadest base of financial support in United States history, largely due to the financing he received from millions of small contributions through the Internet.

The Internet can also compensate for a growing problem in all news media—the concentration of ownership of television stations, newspapers and news sources in the hands of relatively few people. On the Internet, anyone can make available points of view that may be missing from the media. Anyone with word searches can locate websites, blogs or similar online forums that discuss specified issues. When significant events occur almost anywhere in the world, on-site observers can send their reports via the Internet. We no longer have to rely on reporters hired by media conglomerates which may have a political bias that limits what the reporters can say. Similarly, on-site internet communications from places under the control of tyrannical governments can sometimes evade government censorship.

In these ways, the Internet has the potential to be a major democratizing force, not only in the United States but throughout the world. What is required is that people use it to gain information, seek out different points of view, and contribute to the causes and candidates of their choosing. In this way the Internet becomes a generally available alternative means of enabling ordinary citizens to become educated independently of narrowly controlled media conglomerates and independently of governmental control. The Internet also can enable the general public to have a convenient on-line way to provide financial support for the causes and candidates they support. In this way, the disproportionate political influence of wealth can be minimized. An unfettered Internet, thus, is a vital means of enabling the free interchange of information and points of view that the free speech clause of the First Amendment was originally designed to protect.

The need for information and exchange of points of view does not have national boundaries. People within our nation need information and points of view from outside the nation in order to be informed about the potential international effects of the policies of our governmental officials and political candidates. Such information is crucial for the citizens of a democratic society to make informed decisions. The Internet provides access to such information, but only if the international source of the information is not thwarted or restricted by governmental control of the Internet. Thus, we have an interest in supporting every effort to remove any control other governments may have over the Internet. Such control amounts to a violation of human rights—both the human rights of the people subject to restrictions on use of the Internet, and our right and the rights of others to be properly informed by receiving uncensored information from anywhere in the world.

Take Equality Seriously—Without Regard to Gender and Choice of Partner

Democratic values require that we take equality seriously, without regard to ethnicity, nationality, religion, choice of partners, or other means of grouping people in ways that disadvantage them.

I will not rehash here America's sordid history of discrimination and oppression based on perceived differences of race and ethnicity. We know the basics of this history. What we must realize is that America's claim to be a democracy was discredited by this history. The claim continues to be weakened to the extent such discrimination continues to exist, as it still does.

A new frontier for equality is the treatment of "gays." Many states have made it illegal to recognize same-gender relationships. In the name of "family values," most states will not support same-gender families. In short, "family values" has become an excuse to discriminate against gays. "Family values" so construed are not family values at all, but an anti-democratic carryover from the past. Families in a democracy may be same-gender or male-female, and same-gender marriages are of equal value and deserving of equal respect and equal legal protection as male-female marriages. If we take democratic values seriously, we must take equality seriously. Same-gender couples should be treated the same as male-female couples.

To refuse to grant this equality is to discriminate against those who do not choose the opposite gender as their partners. This is a form of discrimination based on gender. Laws prohibiting same-gender marriages or other recognition of same-gender relationships mean that if a person chooses a partner of the same gender, that person will be treated differently and less favorably than if that person had chosen a partner of the opposite gender. That person, thus, is discriminated against based on the gender of the partner. In addition, the same-gender partner is being discriminated against for the same reason.

U.S. federal law currently supports this discrimination against same-gender couples. The federal Defense of Marriage Act,[95] for the purpose of federal funding, defines marriage as existing only between a man and a woman. While this law cannot prevent states from allowing same-gender marriages, it affects federal funding of any benefits that takes marriage into consideration. This federal law is a direct attack on democratic values. It is also a form of discrimination based on gender. (The constitutionality of this law is currently the subject of litigation.)

In addition, laws that prevent the acknowledgment of same-gender couples are examples of dangerous governmental intrusions into our private lives, where personal choice of one's partner should remain the province of the individual and be immune from government control. Ironically, many who oppose "big government" support this governmental intrusion into our personal lives.

Not too long ago, in most states you would be treated differently if you chose as your partner someone considered to be of another "race." As late as 1950, thirty states had laws prohibiting marriages between whites and variously defined non-whites. It was not until 1948 that the highest court of a state called such laws unconstitutional. But in the years following that decision by the Supreme Court of California, applicable at that time only to California, only a minority of those thirty states repealed laws against interracial marriage. It was not until 1967 that the U.S. Supreme Court called such laws unconstitutional. As late as 1967, such laws were openly defended by lawmakers as preventing the pollution of the white race by inferior people, a view then upheld by the Supreme Court of Virginia.[96]

In overturning such laws in 1948, the Supreme Court of California made it clear that "marriage is thus something more than a civil contract subject to regulation by the state; it is a fundamental right of free men."[97] "Legislation infringing such rights must be based upon more than prejudice and must be free from oppressive discrimination to comply with the constitutional requirements of due process and equal protection of the laws."[98] In 1967 the United States Supreme Court stated, "The freedom to marry has long been recognized as one of the vital personal rights essential to the orderly pursuit of happiness by free men. Marriage is one of the 'basic civil rights of man,' fundamental to our very existence and survival."[99]

The principle of democracy, that all people are created equal, has guided the nation to help it overcome, at least partially, over two hundred years of discrimination against nonwhites and women. The principle of democracy has survived and altered the prevailing practices. In overturning laws preventing interracial marriages, the nation's highest court followed the principle of democracy to change age-old anti-democratic social practices and prejudices. In time, that same understanding of marriage that led to the banning of laws against interracial marriages will guide the nation and other nations to overcome discrimination against same-gender marriages. A few states in the United States and several other countries are leading the way. We must understand, however, that every year this discrimination is incorporated into the laws of most of the nation, the nation's claim to be a full democracy is undermined.

Take Equality Seriously—Give Women Full Rights to Their Bodies

What has been called a woman's right to choose whether or not to have an abortion involves more than her right to choose. It involves whether a woman has the same right against governmental intrusion into her life as a man.

Women are different from men, of course, in that inside their bodies could reside a live and viable fetus, while men are deficient in this respect. To use this difference to reduce a woman's right to govern her own body, however, is to use her capacity to bear children against her.

The threatening danger for women is the so-called "pro-life" metaphysical view that "life" begins at conception.

Logically that would mean that the life of a fetus, from day one, must be given the same rights and privileges as any other life. That view would make a pregnant woman, even before she knows she is pregnant, the legal protector of a human being inside of her body.

Current law protects the lives of children. This body of law sees parents as responsible for the well-being of their children. If a child dies due to the negligence of the parents, the parents may be criminally liable. If a child is not properly taken care of or abused, the state can step in and take the child from the parents and have the child raised by foster parents chosen by the state. The laws that protect the child do not have the necessary consequence of treating female parents differently from male parents.

The "pro-life" view, however, would logically extend this body of law to the fetus, beginning with conception. Since the fetus resides only within females, only women would be affected. The logical consequence of the pro-life view is that a woman who carries a fetus is a parent who has the same obligation toward the fetus as a parent has toward a child. It then follows that a woman who has an abortion would be a murderer, for which the woman could, in many states, be executed. If the fetus dies without an abortion, the carrier of the fetus potentially could be subject to criminal prosecution for treating the fetus negligently.

At a time when medical technology can eventually find ways to grow a fertilized egg outside a woman's body, or to remove it from one woman and implant it into another, a logical consequence of the "pro-life" view would give government the same right to remove a fertilized egg from a woman's body to protect it that it has now to remove a child from a home to protect the child. Any pregnant woman who is not in good health as determined by the government, or who expresses misgivings about carrying the fertilized egg until it is born, would be at risk for this kind of governmental intrusion into her body. A woman suspected of wanting to have an abortion, or who has a poor diet or takes certain drugs, could be forced to have her fetus removed for its protection. This is the logical consequence of the "pro-life" view combined with advancement of medical technology.

But the "pro-life" view has other consequences as well. Women usually do not know whether they are pregnant until several weeks into the pregnancy. The "pro-life" view regards the fetus as a living being from conception, which is before the pregnant woman knows that she is pregnant. Logically, the "pro-life" view means that government would be obligated to protect the fertilized egg as soon as it is fertilized in the same way that the government protects children. To accomplish this, the government would have to monitor every woman of child-bearing age and either monitor their sexual activity or subject them to regular examinations to determine whether they are carrying a fertilized egg. Then, once the fertilized egg is detected, the pregnant woman's way of living would be subject to governmental oversight and her mental state would have to be examined to determine her willingness to carry the fetus until it is born. She would be instructed on how to live to preserve the fetus, and any intentional failure to follow these instructions would potentially subject her to criminal prosecution and, if the fertilized egg dies, potentially the death penalty. Though this seems quite extreme, it is nonetheless the ultimate logical consequence of the "pro-life" view, a consequence appropriate for a horrifying tale of science fiction—but this potential is not fiction.

The "pro-life" view, based in religion and metaphysics, has this potential to demean the value of the life of every woman of child-bearing age by taking away her control of her own body. Her ability to pursue life, liberty and the pursuit of happiness would be restricted by the government's concern that she might be carrying a fetus. Instead of "all people are created equal," we would have "all males, and all women who are physically unable to become pregnant, are equal," but other women's lives must be subordinated to the government's desire to protect the unborn. Instead of democracy, we would have a bit of fascism that subordinates women's individuality to the needs of society more than men, simply because of women's ability to become pregnant. Gone would be her individual liberty as long as she is capable of becoming pregnant. In short, "pro-life" is anti-life for women.

If a government, state or federal, adopted the "pro-life" view, it would also be affirming the metaphysical and religious underpinnings of that view. Governments should not be engaged in forming policies based in metaphysics and religion. The lives of women are at stake, not only their well-being but also the actual lives that would be lost due to badly performed underground abortions that would have been declared illegal (since all abortions would be declared illegal). These lives should not be sacrificed on the altar of religious doctrine, a doctrine that would be imposed on those who do not agree with it.

Women's right to their own bodies is currently protected—to some extent—by the U.S. Supreme Court decision in *Roe v. Wade*.[100] But *Roe v. Wade* provides only a transitory and partial protection. *Roe v. Wade* explicitly allows the government to intrude after the first trimester and to intrude to the point of prohibiting abortion the moment the fetus is determined to be viable—that is, capable of living outside the woman's body even with artificial support. The rationale for *Roe v. Wade* depends on this idea of "viability," referred to in the decision as meaning "potentially able to live outside the mother's womb, albeit with artificial aid."[101] The Court admitted that marking the point of viability at the end of the first trimester is "in the light of present medical knowledge."[102] That was in 1973. Advances in medical science have already made the point of viability much sooner. In time, a fertilized egg will be viable upon conception, for there will be and already are ways to grow a fertilized egg into a child.

Thus, *Roe v. Wade* is incorrectly viewed by many as adequate protection for women. By hinging women's liberty on the concept of the "viability" of the fetus, the court decision in that case provided only a temporary and rapidly diminishing protection of a woman's right to her own body—and that temporary protection diminishes further with every medical advance. To keep the "pro-life" movement from gaining enough momentum to overturn that important decision and make matter worse, we must reframe the issue as the right of women to the same dominion over their own bodies as enjoyed by men, a right that is not diminished by pregnancy or the capacity for pregnancy. Any lesser approach would reduce women to being biological pawns of society, leaving them with far fewer rights and liberties than those enjoyed by men.

A progressive legal solution to replace *Roe v. Wade* is to make the pregnant woman the presumed sole prenatal "health care proxy" for the fetus. Many laws now allow health care proxies to make ultimate medical decisions for adults who cannot themselves make decisions due to severe mental impairments. These laws allow for the proxy's judgment legally to determine when life support can be removed to allow a person to die naturally. The proxy who complies with these laws cannot be held liable or prosecuted for this decision. This proposed solution would make the pregnant woman the presumed sole, unrestricted health care proxy that provides the medical decisions for the fetus within her. This presumption would give the pregnant women the full right to decide whether to remove the fetus from the life support that is her own body.

Taking this approach, we can replace the weak decision in *Roe v. Wade* by eliminating the concept of viability altogether. Under this approach, government has no right to intrude into the relationship between a woman and a fetus within her. Governmental actions to provide for the well-being of children cannot occur prior to the child's birth. Upon the child's birth, the presumption that the mother is the sole, unrestricted health care proxy would end.

This solution gives pregnant women their full rights to their bodies during pregnancy, which *Roe v. Wade* does not do. It also places upon them individually the exclusive responsibility for caring for the fetus. This approach—making the pregnant women the presumed sole, unrestricted health care proxy for the fetus within her—shifts the burden of caring for the fetus from government to the individual, where the burden belongs. This solution also avoids making metaphysical or religious assumptions about when life begins. Such assumptions are left up to the individual conscience.

This solution could be reasonably viewed as constitutionally required by the Equal Protection Clause of the Fourteenth Amendment of the U.S. Constitution, by interpreting it to give women the same dominion over their own bodies as enjoyed by men. While it may be a long time before the currently conservative, predominantly male U.S. Supreme Court would seriously consider this approach, this conservative body at least might increasingly allow states to determine a wider scope of women's rights. Most states have constitutional provisions that explicitly or implicitly provide for equal protection of its citizens. Thus, we should be prepared to fight the legal battle in the state courts, based on provisions of state constitutions. Although states cannot take away rights protected by the U.S. Constitution, they can add their own protections beyond what the U.S. Constitution provides.

Objections to this approach may well be based on men's unconscious fear of women's power to create life with only momentary male participation. It is time men faced this fear directly. Male theologies and philosophies over many centuries have sought to usurp this power in favor of male domination, including male domination of marriage and of political, economic, legal and particularly religious institutions. Hierarchical civilizations have been built based on these male ways of thinking. Democratic values require a radically different approach, one that recognizes and accepts women's natural power over the creation of life and does not seek to control this power by reducing pregnant women to pawns of society's desire to maintain itself. This recognition is not something to expect from the predominantly male U.S. Supreme Court. Thus, the government's purported interest in fetal life may be little more than a ruse by men to maintain control over women's natural power, a power that men traditionally have tried to usurp by controlling the lives of women.

While *Roe v. Wade* is defended as protecting women's rights—and to some extent it has—that 1973 opinion by an all-male court was unable to give full respect to women. Instead, it relegated the decision whether to have an abortion during the first trimester to the physician.[103] In 1973, the vast majority of physicians were men. Under that court decision, the state's legitimate interest in the fetus increases after the first trimester. The state's legal interest was controlled at that time, and often still today, by male-dominated legislatures and male-dominated courts. Thus, even *Roe v. Wade* reflects the reluctance of men—often unconscious—to give up their traditional dominance over women.

Until we fully realize that democratic values mean that women are entitled to every right, privilege and immunity enjoyed by men—not just in lip service but in practice—we still have a long way to go to become a fully democratic society.

Take Equality Seriously—Abolish the Death Penalty

All people are not created equal if some people have the legal right to kill another person who is not actively engaged in endangering the life of another. The death penalty is such a legal right. It enables a few decision makers legally to kill a person who has been captured and rendered harmless by imprisonment. The decision makers have superior rights, the right to determine whether the prisoner lives or dies. The prisoner's life has been deprived of any value. The prisoner is the slave of the decision makers and treated as having no right to life. This situation is a blatant denial of the principle of democracy, that all people are created equal. *A fully democratic society cannot have a death penalty.* A society that has a death penalty is not a full democracy.

The death penalty is a total denial of equal rights, whether or not the prisoner is actually guilty. Arguments about the fallibility of human judgment in determining guilt or innocence miss the point. To decide that a prisoner rendered harmless by imprisonment must die is to totally deny the prisoner any rights whatsoever, whether the prisoner is guilty or not. It is this denial of equal right to life that is contrary to democratic values. We cannot consistently affirm that all people are created equal and at the same time have an exception that says, "Unless you do something that appalls us, in which case we can kill you."

As to the act of imprisonment, which is a restriction on the rights of the prisoner, this can be justified as the people's right to protect themselves. People have a right to protect themselves from those whose criminal behavior indicates that they would commit crimes that deny others their equal rights. Thus, imprisonment can be justified to protect the public from harm, but only to the extent necessary for this limited purpose. Once a person has been rendered harmless by imprisonment, killing the prisoner does nothing to protect others. Bad treatment of a prisoner, beyond the act of humane confinement, cannot be justified. The death penalty is the most extreme and cruelest form of bad treatment.

Internationalize Equality

Whenever American politicians say "God bless America," we must remind them that this suggests the provincial view that "God" has a nationalistic point of view, that "He" will favor some people over others, and that the favored people should be ourselves, defined by our nationality, and that our nation should be specially blessed, just as former president George W. Bush believed. What kind of "God" is this? Such a "God" is without universality. Such a "God" is nothing more than an imagined being created in the minds of those who have lost their understanding of democracy, for such a "God" would disrespect democratic values by favoring the people of one nation over another. If the name of God is to be invoked at all, it should be the God who blesses everyone and every nation, not just America.

As explained in Chapter 3, former president George W. Bush led the nation to war on the premise that God favored America. Not only was this a provincial anti-democratic theology, it was a strategic blunder. The stated target was a group without nationality, but Mr. Bush was unable to think in other than nationalistic terms, so he invaded a nation that was irrelevant to that target.

Equality is without borders. "All people are created equal" means "all people," regardless of nationality, gender, ethnicity, religion, age, or sexual orientation. (I did not mention "race" here, because "race" is a mythical creation of the human imagination, having no basis in biology. There is no "race" gene. It is long past the time when the concept of "race" should be totally extinguished from our way of thinking.[104])

This means that we value the life of every Iraqi who died as the result of the American invasion as much as we value the life of an American soldier, regardless of whose side the Iraqi fought on or whether or not he or she was an innocent civilian or a fighter. This means we do not celebrate the killing of a "suspected terrorist," for, first of all, the person has not been found guilty through legal means, and second, the death penalty is itself contrary to democratic values. What is true for Iraqis is true for any nationality and any "suspected terrorist."

Internationalizing equality does not mean ignoring the reality of conflict. But it means taking a different approach that equally values the lives of all people regardless of nationality. Valuing every life equally does not lead to pacifism, but it does lead to a significant reduction in the number of circumstances in which violence can be justified. Classic pacifism does not sufficiently value the life of the pacifist. The classic pacifist philosophy requires those who accept it not to protect themselves by action that might kill an attacker. Those following this philosophy would rather be killed than kill, but that means they devalue their own lives when faced with a violent attacker.

Democratic values mean we value our own lives as much as that of others. We are not less than equal. It means we do what is necessary to protect ourselves from harm or death, because our own lives are precious. If faced with an attack, we may not have time to calculate how best to defend ourselves without fatally harming the attackers. Escape is not always possible. To refuse to defend ourselves would be to devalue our own lives, which is contrary to democratic values, for it would give the attackers greater value than those attacked.

The problems of war and preparation for war and threats of attack are too complex to address here, but democratic values can guide us in finding the solutions. Respect the enemy as human beings whose lives are equal to our own, but do not respect the enemy to the extent you devalue your own safety. It is quite unlikely that democratic values can ever justify being the aggressor or the invader. But democratic values can justify doing what is necessary to protect ourselves in the event others attack. They can certainly justify nonlethal preemptive action. They certainly support attempts at nonviolent solutions including the democratic process of mediation. But preemptive actions that are intended to kill stand on the same ground as the death penalty. They devalue the lives of the other. We cannot devalue others without being the enemy of democratic values.

To affirm democratic values means that whatever makes some different from others does not mean that there is a difference in the value of their lives. It means to think internationally when it comes to valuing people's lives and to regard the valuing of ourselves and others in terms of nationality as an artifact of pre-democratic history, as a variation of ancient tribalism that the future must overcome.

Engage in Progress Toward Greater Democracy

This chapter contains a short selection of the numerous things that must be done to advance toward fuller democracy. The exclusion of any measure from this chapter is not intended to devalue what has been excluded. We cannot know today everything that must be done, any more than did those who lived before us. But we can do what makes sense to affirm democratic values, knowing that whatever we do will help but that what we do will not be enough.

The responsibility for acting is on each of our shoulders, and equally so. In whatever ways we can advance democratic values, we must act to advance them as we seek to create a more humane social and political environment for people throughout the world.

Chapter 6

What We Must Do to Affirm Democratic Values by Building a Caring Society

> *The so-called "golden rule," properly understood, is the ethical source of democratic values.*

Democratic values are rooted in an ethical principle that has been called "the golden rule."[105] This principle has been recognized in various forms for well over two thousand years in all parts of the world. It is not tied to any particular religion or philosophy. It has been voiced in many religions and also in nonreligious philosophies. It provides humankind with its soundest ethical foundation for personal, social and political guidance and growth.

To understand why it is the source of democratic values, we first need to address a common misunderstanding. This broad ethical principle has been called a "rule," thereby implying not only that it is rigid, but also that it has only a personal application and has nothing to do with social or political policy. Neither is true. For reasons that will be clarified later in this chapter, I will abandon calling this principle a "rule" and instead call it the *golden guide*, for it is a complex and flexible ethical principle that provides personal, social and political direction and guidance, not a simplistic, rigid moral rule limited to our personal lives.

The golden guide itself is not just a conceptual abstraction but is rooted in the caring instincts and feelings residing within each of us. Understanding these links will enable us to see how democratic values and democracy are directed toward building a caring society.

The golden guide is often over-simplified, misunderstood or distorted. To understand it and its subtleties, we must carefully interpret it and be able to identify its distortions. Dispelling these distortions is essential to understanding the connection between the golden guide and democratic values and to seeing the life-fulfilling purpose of democracy.

What Is the Golden Guide and Where Does It Come From?

One of the most common formulations of the golden guide is simply, "Do unto others as you would have them do unto you." Throughout most of the history of the recorded thinking of philosophers and religious leaders, we can find some version of the golden guide, sometimes stated narrowly, sometimes broadly. Versions of the golden guide were expressed and affirmed by Confucius and Confucian followers; by the ancient Greek philosophers Thales, Isocrates, Socrates, Plato, and Aristotle; by the Stoics; by Rabbi Hillel; by Jesus; by Christian theologians such as Thomas Aquinas and Martin Luther; by philosophers John Locke and John Stuart Mill; and in Native American lore, just to name a few examples. Versions of it can be found in Hinduism, Confucianism,

Christianity and Islam, and perhaps in other religious traditions as well. No one religious or philosophical tradition can lay exclusive claim to it. It is a broadly accepted ethical principle that many have affirmed as the foundation or core of all moral values.[106]

Yet, there is no one formulation of the golden guide. (One investigator found over 4000 variations.)[107] Various phrasings include "Do not impose on others what you do not desire others to impose upon you,"[108] "Love . . . your neighbor as yourself,"[109] and some contemporary attempts at precision, such as, and "Don't combine (1) acting to do A to X, and (2) not consenting to the idea of A being done to you in an exactly similar situation,"[110] and "If A is rational about rule R, then if there are reasons for A to think R applies to others' conduct toward A, and A is similar to those others in relevant respects, then there are reason for A to think R applies to A's conduct toward others."[111]

The later attempts at precision, however, are no more precise and necessarily leave a degree of ambiguity. These attempts at precision leave questions: What does "rational" mean? How does one determine what are "relevant respects" or an "exactly similar situation"? Thus, each formulation contains a degree of ambiguity, as it should be for an ethical principle that has broad application and is not a rigid rule. This degree of ambiguity is necessary to provide the desired flexibility that is necessary to deal with complex situations and unforeseeable situations. This flexibility allows it to be an ethical guide for addressing such situations, not a rule that would dictate a simple "yes" or "no" answer.

Thus, a range of flexibility is inherent in any formulation of the golden guide. This flexibility allows for there to be more than one desirable way to address a complex situation. Yet, we can see that each formulation is pointing toward a common meaning that evades precise formulation. It is this common meaning, not any particular formulation, that has been widely accepted throughout recorded history and all over the world as a primary principle of ethical values.

But the golden guide is not and cannot be an inflexible "rule" that provides simple "yes" or "no" answers. Seeing it as a rigid "rule" is a primary source of its misinterpretation and distortion.

Misinterpretations of the Golden Guide and its False "Refutations"

When the flexibility inherent in the golden guide is ignored, it becomes easier to misinterpret it as simplistically prescribing only one possible outcome for any situation. Once it is misinterpreted in this way, it is easy to "refute" it by hypothetical counterexamples that show that the golden guide does not work. While some "refutations" are done lightly and need not be taken seriously, some require careful thought and a carefully considered response.

One of the most notable critics of the golden guide was the renowned philosopher Immanuel Kant. His criticisms exemplify many of those made by the golden guide's detractors. One of his criticisms was that golden guide did not correctly or sufficiently prescribe one's duties. He said, "Many a one would gladly consent that others should not benefit him, provided only that he might be excused from showing benevolence to them."[112] In other words, if I would not have another help me, I excuse myself from helping the other.

But this is a superficial way of applying the golden guide. It is superficial, because it does not take into consideration the wants or needs of either the person applying the guide or those of the other. If you take these wants or needs into consideration, the golden guide would lead us to say not what Kant would have it say, but instead, "I would have another not help me only if I do not want or need the other to help me, so I will not help the other only if the other does not want or need help from me." By taking the wants and needs of both self and other into consideration, we apply the golden guide in a way that is fully respectful of both. My refusing to help another who wants or needs help is not excused by my not wanting or needing help. Thus, Kant's criticism fails if we interpret the guide thoughtfully.

Kant's other criticism is also a result of viewing the golden guide superficially and too narrowly. He states, "For on this principle the criminal might argue against the judge who punishes him, and so on."[113] In other words, Kant assumes the person acting as judge who relies on the golden guide would not order punishment for the criminal since if their positions were reversed, the judge (in the position of the criminal) would not want the criminal (in the position of a judge) to order the punishment.

But this supposes that the judge is derelict in fulfilling his duties as a judge. If the judge views himself or herself as upholding equal treatment under the law, which is what the judge has sworn to do in accepting the office, the judge would quite readily concede that if he or she as judge had committed the crime, the punishment should follow.

Thus, if I were the judge following the golden guide, I as judge would apply the law to the criminal as I would have another judge apply the law to me if I had committed the crime. Further, a judge's actions as a judge are not just toward particular criminals but affect the whole citizenry that depends on protection from criminal behavior. In applying the golden guide, I as judge would act toward the citizenry as I would want any member of the citizenry to act toward me, namely to act in accordance with the laws I have vowed as judge to uphold. In addition, my action as a judge affects the effectiveness of other judges. If I as judge don't act in accordance with law, it casts dishonor on the role of judge, adversely affecting other judges. In following the golden guide, I as judge would act toward other judges as I would want other judges to act toward me, namely, by ruling in accordance with law. Thus, as a judge following the golden guide, I would want the law to be applied to me in the same manner as I apply it to others, for this is what it means to uphold compliance with law.

Thus, Kant's criticisms do not succeed. One of his failures was to reduce the golden guide to a bi-directional relationship between one person and another. This is a common error. Instead, the golden guide pertains to a network of relationships between and among one person and all who are affected by that person's actions. The situation of the judge shows some of the complexity of these networks of relationships.[114] These networks of relationships were ignored by Kant, and that is why his critique of the golden guide was simplistic and wrong.

Another superficial interpretation of the golden guide, but also a common one, would have it tell you to do what others *want* you to do. A version of this superficial interpretation is suggested in Herman Melville's *Moby-Dick*. Ishmael considers the request of his friend to engage in an idolatrous religious practice that is contrary to Ishmael's own beliefs. Ishmael first assumes that the will of God is "to do to my fellow man what I would have my fellow man to do me"—one formulation of the golden guide. He then reasons: "Queequeg," his new friend, "is my fellow man. And what do I wish that this Queequeg would do to me? Why, unite with me in my particular Presbyterian form of worship. Consequently, I must then unite with him in his; ergo, I must turn idolator."[115]

What Ishmael proposes here, if viewed as a variation on the golden guide, would turn the golden guide into an obligation to do whatever the other wants—or to justify having done what the other wants. Thus, the golden guide would get distorted to make it an obligation to do unto the other what the other wants if you would want the other to do what you want. But having mutual or reciprocal wants is not the same thing as being obligated to act on those wants. For example, if Maria says she wants to have sex with me, and I would like to have sex with her, it does not follow that I am obligated to have sex with her. Ishmael's reasoning is wrong because it transforms reciprocal wishes or wants into an obligation. Queequeg wants Ishmael to worship as Queequeg worships, and Ishmael wants Queequeg to worship as Ishmael worships, so Ishmael concludes that he "must" do what Queequeg's wants. The transformation of wants, wishes and desires into obligatory actions is not required or implied by the golden guide. "Do unto others as you would have them do unto you" does not contain an obligation to do unto others what they would want you to do even if you would want them to do the same thing. There may be other good reasons not to do what another wants. Given the complexity of most real-life situations, rarely would the golden guide require only one possible course of action.

The transformation of wants between two people into an obligation, while erroneous in itself, also narrows the golden guide into a simple bi-lateral relationship between two people and does not consider others beyond the pair. But the golden guide is not just about me and another, or the other and me. Instead, it pertains to our interactions with any others who are affected by our actions. The effects we have on others mean there are likely to be other reasons not to act on mutual wants and desires between two people. Thus, instead of me and Maria acting on our mutual wants, I would consider the affects of my actions on others. I may be married to someone else, and in applying the golden guide to my relationship with her, I may decide that I want to be faithful to her more than I want to have sex with Maria. Or, Maria might be married to my best friend, and applying the golden guide to my relationship with him, I may decide that upsetting my best friend is sufficient reason not to have sex with Maria.

There may be other reasons as well. Just because two people want the same things from each other does not mean they must or should act on what they want. In this example, I must also apply the golden guide to my wife, or my best friend, and to any others who would also be affected by my relationship with Maria, and not do unto them what I would not want them to do unto me.

Had Ishmael correctly applied the golden guide, he might instead have reasoned, "Queequeg wants me to join him in his worship. I would want him to join me in my worship. But I would want him to respect my decision not to join him in his worship, so I will respect his decision not to join me in my worship." This leaves Ishmael free to act in accordance with his conscience, just as he would also leave Queequeg free to act in accordance with his conscience. We then see that neither is obligated to take the action that the other wants, and, similarly, that the golden guide cannot be used to justify such actions.

The prevalence of various "refutations" and misuse of the golden guide, such as those just considered, indicate that the golden guide can be easily misinterpreted or applied superficially. These misinterpretations of the golden guide result from over-simplification or lack of thoughtfulness in formulating and applying the guide. Using the golden guide requires careful interpretation and application, including a recognition that an action toward one person may also affect others. It is not just a guide for relating to our neighbors, it is also a guide for considering the broader effects of our actions on all who are affected by them.

Thus, we must be cautious and skeptical if we too quickly conclude the golden guide justifies something we want to do or have done, or if it seems to justify something that seems clearly wrong. If either happens, it may be because we are interpreting the golden guide too narrowly. The golden guide pertains to our networks of relationships where simple answers are unlikely. Nonetheless, it is a guide that gives us direction for figuring out the best course of action.

It is Not a "Rule" But a Guide

Many would like morality to be reduced to a set of simple rules or commandments to be followed at all times. They want to say with certainty that *this* is always right and *that* is always wrong. The only way this can be done is to ignore the complexities and uncertainties of life. The golden guide, properly interpreted, does not provide simple answers that ignore these complexities and uncertainties. Thus, it cannot be reduced to a rule and should not be called a rule.

The golden guide was not originally called a "rule." The popularization of the term "golden rule" apparently began in the seventeenth century due to the writings of four Englishmen who most likely were seeking moral certainty and simplicity.[116] The golden guide, however, goes back many centuries before that. Whatever the motive may have been in the seventeenth century to call it a "rule," today's common use of the term "rule" suggests a clarity and rigidity that is not appropriate for the general ethical principle that the golden guide expresses. It is time to question the designation given by these Englishmen over three centuries ago.

Rules are ordinarily seen as stating clearly what should and should not be done. "No smoking" is a rule of many places, and it is clear when the rule is broken. Condominium associations have more complicated rules, but they generally consist of clearly stated "do's" and "don't's." Rules are generally written to state clearly what is permitted and what is not.   In addition to simply stating what is and is not permitted, a "rule" is generally something that we think justifies some kind of punishment for those who break it. It is imposed on those who disagree with it, since those who disagree with it must, if they cannot change it, either follow it or have punishment imposed upon them if they break it.

The golden guide, unlike a rule, cannot be imposed on others under threat of penalty or punishment. Why? Because if you believe that you do not want others to impose on you a moral principle that you believe is wrong, then, if you accept the golden guide, you would not want to impose on others a moral principle that they believe is wrong. Consequently, you cannot impose the golden guide on others if they do not accept it, and you cannot punish others for not accepting it.

The golden guide, thus, should not be analogized to a rule or law. Rules and laws are different. The functioning of modern society requires enforced laws, ideally ones adopted through democratic processes. As long as democratic processes allow for changing the laws, we accept the requirements of law as necessary and fair. We agree to follow laws we do not agree with as long as we believe that the law was created through legitimate means, or that following laws generally is a good idea. We also generally agree to follow laws we do not agree with, because we think we have the opportunity to change the laws through some fair process. Those who disobey the law are subject to some form of fair punishment.

The golden guide is not like a law. As explained above, we cannot legitimately impose the golden guide on those who reject it without acting against the golden guide. Thus, the golden guide is not a law or rule to impose on others but a guide for our own living. To treat it as a "rule" is to misunderstand it.

The Golden Guide as the Source of Democratic Values

"Do unto others as you would have them do unto you" guides us to see others as of equal worth to ourselves. It says, in effect, that others deserve the same treatment you would want for yourself. Our equality to others, and theirs to us, is clearly implied.

While the golden guide does not explicitly state that "all people are of equal worth," we can perform this mental experiment to show that this is what the golden guide means:

> *Ask yourself, Who are the "others" you are to "do unto as you would have them do unto you"? Presumably it includes those with whom you have a relationship. It could be your spouse, your child, neighbors, other family members, colleagues, or any others with whom you interact. They constitute the circle of "others" to whom you would apply the golden guide, a circle which usually changes over time. If you believe you should use the golden guide in relating to them, this circle consists of those whom you would treat as though they were of equal worth to yourself, for in applying the golden guide you would be treating*

them as you would have them treat you.

But consider how this circle, through others, continually expands beyond those you personally know or interact with.

To see how this happens, pretend one of these others in your circle is your friend, Samuel. Thus, Samuel is one of those whom you consider to be of equal worth to you. You would want Samuel to use the golden guide for two reasons. First, since you believe the golden guide is a good thing to use, you would want others to use it too (while remembering that you cannot impose it on anyone). Secondly, you would want Samuel to apply the golden rule in his relationship to you, since that would be to your benefit. If Samuel uses the golden guide consistently, he would use it not just for your benefit but also in his relationships to those in his circle similarly to the way you use it in your relationships to those in your circle. Accordingly, Samuel would consider those in his circle to be of equal worth to him.

But Samuel's circle is likely to include some people who are not in your circle. Let's call one of these people in Samuel's circle who is not in your circle, Susan. Since Samuel is using the golden guide in his relationship to Susan, Samuel would treat Susan as though she was of equal worth to him. Thus, you consider yourself equal to Samuel, and Samuel considers himself equal to Susan.

Since you believe that both you and Samuel should use the golden guide, the equality of you and Samuel and the equality of Samuel and Susan reasonably and logically implies the equality of you and Susan. The equality of you and Susan occurs even though Susan is someone you do not know.

You can continue the same process of thinking to

establish the equality of Susan to someone in her circle—call him George—who is not in your or Samuel's circle. You would want Susan to use the golden guide for two reasons. First, since you believe the golden guide is a good thing to use, you would want Susan to use it too. Second, you would want Susan to use the golden guide for Samuel's benefit, for your doing unto Samuel as you would have him do unto you reasonably would include wanting Samuel to be treated by Susan as she would want Samuel to treat her. Thus, you would want Susan to use the golden guide toward those in her circle that includes Samuel. If she does, she would treat those in her circle as though they were of equal worth to her. Since those in Susan's circle include George, and we have already established the equality of you and Susan, it is reasonable and logical to say that you and George also are equals. Both Susan and George are people you never met.

By continuing this line of thinking, you will see that your circle expands into an every-expanding circle that includes the circles of others without limit, so ultimately everyone is included. What began as an application of the golden guide to someone in your circle whom you know and interact with ends up including those you do not know. Thus everyone becomes part of the expanded network of circles of those considered to be of equal worth. "All people are of equal worth" reasonably follows from this train of thought that began with your belief in the golden guide as applied to your circle.

That all people are of equal worth is the core of democratic values. Thus, believing in democratic values reasonably follows from believing in the golden guide. This is why the golden guide is the ethical source of the principle of equality and democracy.

Caring: The Ultimate Source of Democratic Values

Since the golden guide has for more than two millennia been proclaimed cross-culturally and transnationally as the core of all ethical and moral principles, democratic values rest upon an historically firm and broadly based foundation. This foundation is broader than any particular religion and also includes many nonreligious views of ethics and morality.

But while this historical and broad foundation is a good reason for giving the golden guide serious consideration as a primary ethical principle, we should inquire further than this to find the reasons for accepting it. After all, what people may have believed for centuries does not automatically mean that it is true or right. The history of humankind is full of examples of beliefs held for centuries that were false.

Thus, to support the golden guide, we should look further. It is fair to ask, Where does the golden guide come from? Why should I accept it?

We can find the answer in a surprising place—within ourselves. The following mental experiment reveals why:

> *Begin by identifying someone you know personally whom you strongly care about. Let's pretend this person's name is* Jennifer.
>
> *Then ask yourself how you would like to treat Jennifer.*
>
> *If you care about Jennifer, you would not want to do her harm. As you think about how you would want to*

relate to her, it is likely that you would not want to treat her differently from the way you would want to be treated. If you were to put these caring feelings into words, the words would be something like, "I will do unto Jennifer as I would have Jennifer do unto me." This verbalization of the effects of your caring feelings is the first step toward formulating the golden guide.

Next, consider how you would like others to treat Jennifer. Since you deeply care about her, you would want her to be treated by others with caring. The words you used to describe your caring about Jennifer can be applied to how you would like others to treat her: "I want others to do unto her as they would want her to do unto them." Since these others may be anyone without limit, you begin to see how the golden guide has a general applicability that is much broader than just your relationship to Jennifer.

Then consider how your own caring for Jennifer extends even further beyond her. Jennifer is someone within your circle of people with whom you have caring relationships. Jennifer has her own circle of caring relationships, some of which may include someone you do not know. Let's call the person in her caring circle that is not in your caring circle, Jack. Although Jack is someone you do not know, you would want him to treat Jennifer with caring. But Jack's ability to treat Jennifer with caring depends on his well-being. Thus, Jack's well-being becomes something you would care about, because his ability to care for Jennifer depends on it. Whether or not you get to know Jack, you would want to treat Jack with the same caring with which you treat Jennifer, because Jennifer's well being depends in part on Jack's ability to act with caring *towards her. Accordingly, you would want to use the golden guide in your relationship with Jack, just as you would also want Jack to use the golden guide in his relationship with Jennifer.*

This process of thinking does not end, for it extends to others who relate to Jack, and so on, similar to the way the golden guide expands without limit to other circles.

We can now see, through these mental experiments, how our caring feelings for those closest to us, when combined with thoughtfulness about what this means, are the source within us of the golden guide. It is this caring within us that generates the feeling of the worth of the other, and by adding the thoughtful reflection contained in these mental experiments, we can see how this caring extends beyond those we know.

The golden guide, thus, is not a duty imposed on us from outside of us, but a sense of responsibility generated from within us by our own caring desires. Democratic values express this sense of responsibility by recognizing the equal worth of all. Democratic values follow from the awareness that all are involved in interconnected networks of caring: our caring of others, our desire for yet others to treat those we care about with caring, our desire for those others to be treated with caring, and so on. These networks of caring reasonably expand without limit, ultimately embracing everyone.

What gets in the way of this expanded network of caring is the defining of ourselves as a member of a group that is different from other groups, usually combined with a metaphysical view that there is something called "evil" that infects only one or more of the other groups. This metaphysical view, "moralistic dualism," is explained in Chapter 2 and further illuminated with the example in Chapter 3.

But because moralistic dualism is so pervasive in the culture, we have to frequently remind ourselves that those who have beliefs that reflect moralistic dualism are not infected with evil and are not inferior to ourselves. Nonetheless, we have to recognize that moralistic dualism consists of beliefs that are incompatible with democratic values.

Democratic Values Mean Building a Caring Society

Seeing the golden guide as more than a personally held belief and as providing the ethical foundation for democratic values enables us to see the golden guide both as emanating from us as thoughtful caring individuals and also as emanating historically as a world-wide expression of thoughtful caring. As we study the history and prevalence of the golden guide, we will see that we share something that is fundamental and held in common with others living throughout human history and in all parts of the world. Just as the source of the golden guide comes from within each of us, so does the potential source of the golden guide for others come from within each of them. That source is the caring within us expanded beyond us through thoughtful reflection.

These sources of the golden guide do not prove it to be an absolute, universal principle that must be followed by all. Looking for such a proof would miss the point, because, as explained above, the golden guide is not something that can be forcefully imposed on others. When we abandon the illusory mental framework of moralistic dualism, the need to find absolute certainty vanishes, for the goal is to guide ourselves, not to justify the use of force to make others live by what are mistakenly imagined to be absolute rules.

Nonetheless, the awareness that the golden guide is shared cross-culturally and around the world, and that it has been so for many centuries, further strengthens the view that the golden guide is truly a sound ethical principle for daily living and that it provides a sound ethical foundation for an unlimited community seen as an unending network of interlinked and overlapping caring circles. To affirm the golden guide on such a societal basis is to affirm a view of unlimited community where people express their caring for one another by following the golden guide. Democratic values are derived from this view and express it in another form. These values provide the foundation for building a society and a societal infrastructure that supports every individual within it, with the goal of enabling all to live meaningful lives in the pursuit not only of their own happiness but also the happiness of others. This support of every person is what a caring society would provide and what democratic values require.

Though we may initially think of such a society as contained within certain geographical or national boundaries, a caring society based on democratic values has no boundaries. This is the meaning of "All people are created equal." "All people" means just that, without limitation.

Chapter 7

What We Must Do to Resume the Building of a Democratic Framework for Human Growth

> *The growth of democracy is up to us.*

Democracy is not a snapshot of any existing society. Rather, it is a constantly developing societal framework that provides the potential for human growth consistent with the golden guide. This framework is itself subject to change as our growth through history and into the future leads us to understand better what it means to be fully human.

The beginning of a democratic framework in the United States was set up by the Founders. They understood that there is a connection between democratic values and social structure. They began with the rudimentary assertion of democratic values: "All men are created equal." Then they proceeded, as others joined them, to create a constitutional framework designed to incorporate those values. The constitutional framework was wisely designed to give it stability as it also allowed for it to change.

The allowance for change of the framework itself was critical. Through amendments, the Bill of Rights was quickly added. But even with the Bill of Rights, the Constitution nonetheless contained a horrendous flaw. That flaw was slavery. Slavery was acknowledged and accepted in the original Constitution.[117] It was accepted by the same Founders who are often referred to with superficial reverence that fails to acknowledge their human failings. The flaw of slavery was so serious that it could not be removed peacefully. Not until the Civil War was over and hundreds of thousands of lives destroyed could the flaw be partially corrected with the addition of the Thirteenth, Fourteenth, and Fifteenth Amendments. Yet, the constitutional framework itself permitted the amendments and established the means by which they could be added. The framework contained its own mechanisms permitting it to change.

But more changes were needed to bring us to today. For example, the meaning and critical importance of freedom of speech was initially not understood but developed over time.[118] It was not until 1920 that women were guaranteed the right to vote with the addition of the Nineteenth Amendment. The slowly but steadily changing framework over many decades since the Civil War has permitted the growth of a multicultural, multiethnic society that provides a large degree of legal protection against excessive governmental power and has permitted the enactment of laws that constrain individuals, groups and economic powers from oppressing others based on gender, ethnicity and nationality. It has also permitted the enactment of many laws designed to protect civil rights and the equal right to vote by all. In many respects the United States today is far more democratic than the society that existed when the nation was created. We must note, however, that it has taken over two hundred years to make this progress. We would be presumptuous, and wrong, to believe that this progress has reached its conclusion and therefore nothing more needs to be done.

In many respects, democratic values remain confined or unrealized. Women still are denied the constitutional protection of the Equal Rights Amendment, which has not been ratified. Governmental intrusion into our private lives has been incrementally and dangerously increased in the name of security. A significant portion of the population does not have adequate health care or lives below the poverty line. The populace of the United States, as a whole, continues to be disrespectful of others beyond its borders. The popular outcry that began in 2003 against France and French products following France's refusal to join in the invasion of Iraq bespeaks of intolerance toward dissent. The U.S. invasion of Iraq reflects the national tendency to attack and destroy what it does not like, a tendency that began with the intentional destruction of Native American life and culture in this nation's earlier years, and continued in more recent times in its failed attempt to conquer Southeast Asia and its long-standing efforts to control the politics of Latin America, using violence and economic support of the violence of others as its methods. This horrendous legacy still undermines democratic values. More recently the nation has attempted to control the politics of the Middle East, supposedly to expand democracy but more likely to protect financial interests and access to oil. The nation has yet to come to terms with democratic values in its arrogant and aggressive treatment of others outside its national boundaries.

We would be simplistic to call this foreign intrigue and intolerance "wrong" or "immoral." We are faced with conflicting views of what is right and wrong. According to ancient morality, our foreign intrigue and intolerance could be justified as the struggle against evil. Our national leaders make sure ancient morality is called upon when they want to justify war and aggressive dominance over others. The United States invaded Vietnam and Cambodia in the name of fighting the "evil" of communism. The United States invaded Iraq in the name of fighting the "evil" of terrorism. As long as we allow this ancient morality to govern us, we will find "evil" in the form of people to kill, people who are seen as hostile to our interests. Of course, the "evil" is always "them" and not us.

This ancient morality, *moralistic dualism*, underlies the anti-democratic mentality that has dominated most of humankind throughout recorded history. Democratic values lead us in a direction that is quite different, in some cases radically different.

Unlike this ancient morality, the source of democratic values is not a metaphysical belief in the existence of evil that must be destroyed. Instead, for their source we turn to the golden guide, the source of which is not metaphysical but which is generated from our own caring feelings and reasonably expanded through thoughtful reflection.

The golden guide incorporates the principle of equality, the principle that is the core of democratic values. To call another "evil" is to affirm inequality. We cannot consistently adhere to the ancient morality of moralistic dualism and also believe in democratic values. We cannot consistently adhere to this ancient morality and also believe in the golden guide. The golden guide means that we will not call others evil and seek their destruction if we do not want others to call us evil and support our destruction. We cannot consistently call others evil without affirming the same anti-democratic perspective that allows them to call us evil.

In addition, the golden guide cannot be imposed on others through force without violating it. If you do not want others to impose upon you their view of an ethical principle that conflicts with the golden guide, then you cannot impose the golden guide on those who do not accept or follow the golden guide. The golden guide, in other words, is a guide for our own lives, and we cannot legitimately use it as a weapon to force others to live and behave in any particular way. Thus, the golden guide can never be used to justify the existence of a central political or religious authority with military or police power that can be used to force others to comply with the golden guide or any other ideal or principle.

This characteristic of the golden guide further explains the reason for the paradox of democracy, that we cannot impose the principle "all people are of equal worth" on those who do not accept it without violating *their* equal worth. In other words, those who oppose democracy are of equal worth to those who support it. (As explained in Chapter 2, this does not change the need for civil law and a military defense, but it may change how the law is enforced and our understanding of what constitutes defense.)

To put the golden guide and democratic values into practice, we must both proclaim this fundamental framework that makes democracy possible and work within this framework to make democratic values a reality in the way we live and interact with others. Realizing democratic values means not only attaining the goals discussed in Chapter 5 but also furthering the growth of a social, political and cultural environment that respects the equal worth of every person and supports each person in maximizing his or her potential in a way that is consistent with others maximizing their potential. Such an environment would include a social consciousness that respects every faith as personal and not as something to be imposed on others.

While considerable progress has been made in this direction over the course of history, much remains to be done. Complacent acceptance of the existing state of things allows for the resurgence of ancient morality that is anti-democratic. Instead of such acceptance, we must do the work that furthers progress toward a society—and a world community—that maximizes the potential of every person to grow and live productively.

Democracy means that this work is not something we delegate to a ruler or authority but is work that is up to each of us. As Justice Louis Brandeis wrote, "The greatest menace to freedom is an inert people."[119]

NOTES

———————————————

CHAPTER 1

1. John Quincy Adams, *Inaugural Address*, March 4, 1825.

2. The most notable advance in the concept of one person, one vote occurred in the 1960's due to three major decisions of the U.S. Supreme Court that required equitable apportionment of voting districts: *Baker v. Carr,* 369 U.S. 186 (1962), *Wesberry v. Sanders,* 376 U.S. 1(1964), and *Reynolds v. Sims,* 377 U.S. 533 (1964).

3. *Alexander Meiklejohn: Teacher of Freedom*, ed. Cynthia Stokes Brown, Berkeley, CA,: Meiklejohn Civil Liberties Institute, 1981, p. 257.

4. See "U.S. Policy on Terror Suspects Criticized," *Boston Globe*, Nov. 3, 2005, p. A3, col. 5; "GOP Senators Add Heat on Spying," *Boston Globe*, February 7, 2006, p. 1, col. 1.

5. Jeffrey Toobin, *Too Close to Call*, New York: Random House, 2001, p. 180.

6. Toobin, p. 181.

7. *Bush v. Gore,* 531 U.S. 98, 2000. *See* Toobin, *Too Close to Call,* pp. 263 – 67.

8. See report of U.S. Commission on Civil Rights titled, "Voting

Irregularities in Florida During the 2000 Presidential Election," June, 2001 (http://www.usccr.gov/pubs/vote2000/report/main.htm). See Toobin, *Too Close to Call*, pp. 171 - 75 & 281.

9. See Toobin, *Too Close to Call*, pp. 14 - 15, 81, 280 - 81.

10. *What Went Wrong in Ohio: The Conyers Report on the 2004 Presidential Election,* Chicago: Academy Chicago Publishers, 2005.

11. These protests were documented in Michael Moore's film, *Fahrenheit 9/11.*

12. The dissent of Abigail Thernstrom and Russell G. Redenbaugh in "Voting Irregularities in Florida During the 2000 Presidential Election" (which may be found at http://www.thernstrom.com) assumed that a showing of "systemic disenfranchisement" has to be made to question an election. But this was never the legal standard.

13. A seminal case is *Mobile v. Bolden,* 446 U.S. 55 (1980). Justice Marshall's dissent provides an excellent analysis of the potential impact of the court's views.

14. When Jeffrey Toobin in his book, *Too Close to Call, op. cit.,* p. 169, discounts the contention that the state of Florida disenfranchised thousands of black voters, he confused intentional disenfranchisement with disenfranchisement. His own book documents this disenfranchisement, and, as I explain, whether it was intentional or not is beside the moral and ethical point which he himself makes.

15. *What Went Wrong in Ohio, op. cit.*

16. "Florida still can't count all the votes," *The Boston Globe*, Nov. 24, 2006, p. A15, col. 3 – 6; "Fla. judge rules against election challenger," *The Boston Globe*, Dec. 30, 2006, p. A2, col. 2 – 6.

17. Clive Thompson, "Can You Count on Voting Machines?" *The New York Times Magazine*, January 6, 2008.

18. "44% in poll OK limits on rights of Muslims," *The Boston Globe*, December 18, 2004, p. A3, col. 1. "MSRG Special Report: Restrictions on Civil Liberties, Views of Islam, & Muslim Americans," Report of the Media & Society Research Group, Cornell University, December, 2004, p 1.

19. "MRSG Special Report," p. 1.

20. "Firms block gays' benefits, cite US law," *The Boston Globe*, December 18, 2004, p. A1, col. 5 & 6.

21. The report of the study is contained in "Mortality before and after the 2003 invasion of Iraq: cluster sample survey," in *The Lancet*, released online October 29, 2004, by Les Roberts, Riyadh Lafta, Richard Garfield, Jamal Khudhairi and Gilbert Burnham. A discussion of the report was found on the BBC website at http://news.bbc.co.uk/1/hi/world/middle_east/3962969.stm.

22. *The Boston Globe*, July 20, 2005, p. A8, col. 2 - 5.

23. Speech to the Philadelphia World Affairs Council at the Park Hyatt Philadelphia. Quoted from the text that was provided by www.GOP.com.

24. "Iraqis estimate civilian deaths at 150,000," *The Boston Globe*, November 10, 2006, p. A3, col. 1 - 5. See also, Marilynn Marchione, "Study: 151,000 Iraqis killed in first 3 years of war," *The Boston Globe*, January 10, 2008, p. A8, col. 2 – 6.

25. "Disputed study says 600,000 Iraqis killed during war," *The Boston Globe*, October 12, 2006, p. A16, col. 3 - 4.

26. Derrick Z. Jackson, "The Victims We Don't Count," *The Boston Globe*, January 7, 2005, p. A13.

27. See, for example, Stephen Kinzer, *Overthrow: America's Century of Regime Change from Hawaii to Iraq*, New York: Times Books, 2006; Jim Garrison, *America as Empire: Global Leader or Rogue Power*, San Francisco: Berrett-Koehler, 2004.

CHAPTER 2

28. The concepts and much of the historical information discussed here are contained and documented, using somewhat different terminology, in John L. Hodge, D. K. Struckmann & L. D. Trost, *Cultural Bases of Racism and Group Oppression*, Berkeley, California: Two Riders Press, 1975. Similar ideas were also presented in John L. Hodge, "Equality: Beyond Dualism and Oppression," ch. 6 of *Anatomy of Racism*, ed. David Theo Goldberg, Minneapolis: Univ. of Minnesota Press, 1990.

29. A classic study of the history of the ideal of hierarchy is Arthur O. Lovejoy's *The Great Chain of Being*, originally published by Harvard University Press, 1936.

30. See Hodge, et al., *Cultural Bases*, Part I.

31. Newton P. Stallknecht and Robert S. Brumbaugh, *The Spirit of Western Philosophy*, New York: David McKay, 1950, p. *v*.

32. Of course it is not possible to mark a precise starting point of the idea of democratic government as conceived in modern times, but a good estimate would be the publication of John Locke's

influential *Two Treatises of Government* in 1690. It is widely
believed that Locke was "a main source of the ideas of the
American Revolution in 1776." Thomas P. Peardon,
"Introduction," *The Second Treatise of Government*,
Indianapolis: Bobbs-Merrill, 1952. We must also recognize that
democracy in various forms has been conceived in various parts
of the world over many centuries.

33. Aristotle, *Politics*, 1252a.

34. Aristotle, *Politics*, 1254b.

35. Martin Luther, "Temporal Authority: To What Extent It Should
Be Obeyed," trans. J. J. Schindel, rev. W. I. Brandt, *Luther's
Works*, Vol. 45, Philadelphia: Fortress, 1962, p. 88.

36. Ibid., p. 95.

37. John Calvin, *Institutes of the Christian Religion*, trans. F. L.
Battles, 3.14.3; in *The Library of Christian Classics*, Vol. XX &
XXI, Philadelphia: Westminster, 1960.

38. See Hodge, et al., *Cultural Bases*, Part IV.

39. Immanuel Kant, *Education,* trans. Annette Churton, Ann Arbor:
Ann Arbor Paperbacks, 1960, p. 4.

40. Immanuel Kant, *Critique of Practical Reason*, trans. Lewis White
Beck, p. 153 of Prussian Academy Edition, Vol. V; Indianapolis:
Bobbs-Merrill, 1956, p. 156.

41. Immanuel Kant, *Perpetual Peace,* Sec. II, "First Definitive Article
for Perpetual Peace," Indianapolis: Bobbs-Merrill, 1957, p. 14.

42. Sigmund Freud, *The Future of an Illusion*, rev. ed., trans. W. D.
Robson-Scott, Garden City, N.Y: Doubleday, 1964, p. 5.

43. See, for example, Plato, *The Republic,* 466; trans. Desmond Lee, 2nd ed., Baltimore: Penguin Books, 1974, p. 252.

44. Plato, *The Republic,* 431; trans. Desmond Lee, 2nd ed., Baltimore: Penguin Books, 1974, p. 202.

45. Aristotle, *Politics,* 1254b, 1259b, 1260a; *The Basic Works of Aristotle,* ed. Richard McKeon, New York: Random House, 1941, pp. 1132, 1143 & 1144.

46. St. Augustine, *Confessions,* Bk. II, #2, trans. R. S. Pine-Coffin, Baltimore: Penguin, 1961.

47. Martin Luther, "Treatise on Good Works," trans. W. A. Lambert and revised by J. Atkinson, *Luther's Works,* Vol. 44, Philadelphia: Fortress, 1966, p. 98.

48. John Calvin, *The Epistle to the Ephesians,* 5:22. Contained in *Calvin's Commentaries: The Epistles of Paul the Apostle to the Galatians, Ephesians, Philippians and Colossians,* trans. T. H. L. Parker, London: Oliver & Boyd, 1965.

49. *Ibid,* p. 78.

50. *Ibid,* pp. 78 - 81.

51. Sigmund Freud, *Civilization and Its Discontents,* trans. James Strachey, New York: W. W. Norton, 1962, pp. 50 - 51.

52. Sigmund Freud, *An Outline of Psycho-Analysis,* trans. James Strachey, New York: W. W. Norton, 1949, p. 51.

53. Sigmund Freud, "Reflections upon War and Death," trans. E. Colburn Mayne, in *Character and Culture,* ed. Paul Rieff, New York: Collier Books, 1963, p. 108; see also p. 113.

54. Sigmund Freud, *Totem and Taboo*, trans. James Strachey, New York: W. W. Norton, 1950, pp. 2, 3 n.2, 12 ff, 40-41, 54 & 139.

CHAPTER 3

55. The numbers in parentheses correspond to the numbers in the text. The titles and dates of each entry are those that were provided on the websites, GOP.com or whitehouse.gov.
    (1) 9/11/01: "President George W. Bush's Address to the Nation."
    (2) 9/14/01: "The Commitment of our Fathers is Now with Calling of our Time," The National Cathedral, Washington, D.C.
    (3) 9/20/01: "President Bush's Address to a Joint Session of Congress and the Nation."
    (4) 9/24/01: "President Bush Freezes Terrorists' Assets," remarks upon signing an Executive Order.
    (5) 9/25/01: "President Bush Addresses Employees at the FBI," FBI Headquarters, Washington, D.C.
    (6) 10/4/01: "President Directs Humanitarian Aid to Afghanistan," U.S. Department of State, Washington, D.C.
    (7) 10/4/01: "President Bush Proposes Back to Work Relief Package" (location not indicated).
    (8) 10/7/01: "The President's Address To The Nation."
    (9) 10/13/01: "President Bush Reports On The State of War Against Terror," press conference.
    (10) 10/30/01: "President Launches Lessons of Liberty," Thomas Wooten High School, Rockville, Maryland.
    (11) 11/6/01: "No Nation Can Be Neutral in This Conflict," remarks to the Warsaw Conference on Combating Terrorism.
    (12) 11/11/01: "Remarks by the President At Veterans Day Prayer. Breakfast," Park Avenue Seventh Regiment

Armory, New York.
(13) 11/19/01: "President Signs Aviation Security Legislation," Ronald Reagan National Airport, Washington, D.C.
(14) 11/22/01: "Thanksgiving Day Proclamation."
(15) 1/23/02: "Remarks by the President at Reserved Officers Association Luncheon," Washington Hilton Hotel, Washington, D.C.
(16) 1/29/02: "The President's State of the Union Address."
(17) 10/23/02: "President Bush signs Defense Bill to 'Defend Our Freedom,'" remarks upon signing.
(18) 11/11/02: "President Commemorates Veterans Day," at the White House reception for veterans.
(19) 12/2/02: "Bush Signs Defense Budget for a Nation at War," remarks upon signing.
(20) 1/28/03: "President Delivers 'State of the Union.'"
(21) 3/17/03: "President Bush Addresses Nation on Iraqi Threat."
(22) 4/3/03: "President Expresses Gratitude to Servicemen and Women at Camp Lejeune."
(23) 5/1/03: "Presidential Address from USS Lincoln."
(24) 7/30/03: "President Highlights Progress in Achieving National Priorities," press conference.
(25) 1/21/04: "President Bush's State of the Union Address."
(26) 5/6/04: "Remarks By President Bush at 2004 RNC Gala."
(27) 9/2/04: "In Acceptance Speech, Bush Shares His Plan for a Safer World & More Hopeful America" at the Republican National Convention.
(28) 11/3/04: "President Bush Thanks Americans in Acceptance Speech," at the Ronald Reagan Building, Washington, D.C.
(29) 4/12/05: "Remarks By President Bush On The War On Terror," at Fort Hood.
(30) 5/27/05: "Remarks By The President At The United States Naval Academy Commencement."
(31) 6/9/05: "Remarks By The President On The Patriot Act," Columbus, Ohio.
(32) 6/29/05: "President Addresses Nation, Discusses Iraq, War on Terror."

(33) 8/24/05: "Remarks By The President In The War on Terror," before the Idaho National Guard.

(34) 1/23/06: Remarks by the President on the Global War on Terror, Kansas State University, Manhattan, Kansas.

(35) 1/25/06: Release of Office of the Press Secretary, January 25, 2006, "President Visits National Security Agency," Fort Meade, Maryland.

(36) 1/31/06: State of the Union Address.

(37) 9/11/06: President Bush Addresses The Nation.

(38) 9/29/06: Remarks By The President On The Global War On Terror, Washington, D.C.

(39) 1/10/07: President Bush Addresses the Nation on Iraq.

(40) 1/23/07: State of the Union Address.

(41) 4/19/07: Remarks by the President on the Global War on Terror.

(42) 7/21/07: President's Radio Address.

(43) 11/1/07: President Bush Discusses Global War on Terror, at The Heritage Foundation, Washington, D.C.

56. Stated, among other places, "In Acceptance Speech, Bush Shares His Plan for a Safer World & More Hopeful America" at the Republican National Convention, September 2, 2004, and in "President Bush Remarks On Freedom And Democracy," at the White House, March 29, 2005.

57. During his administration, his speeches were available at the Internet websites, www.whitehouse.gov and www.GOP.com, Many of his earlier speeches on war are recorded in the book, *"We Will Prevail": President George W. Bush on War, Terrorism, and Freedom*, ed. by National Review, New York: Continuum International Publishing Group, 2003.

58. See *The Boston Globe*, Nov. 11, 2005, p. A2, col. 2 - 5.

59. See *The Boston Globe*, Nov. 16, 2005, p. A21, col. 1 - 3.

54. Pub.L. No. 109-366 (Oct. 17, 2006): Section 3 of the Act inserted Chapter 47A into Subtitle A of Title 10 of the United States Code; section 948a(1)(A)(i) of Chapter 47A defines an unlawful enemy combatant, who may a legal alien or visitor, as any "person who has engaged in hostilities or who has purposefully and materially supported hostilities against the United States or its co-belligerent"; section 948d(c) gives the President or his appointees full authority to determine who is an unlawful enemy combatant without judicial review. Section 7 of the Act replaces a provision in section 2241(e) of Title 28 of the U.S. Code and denies the writ of habeas corpus not only to "unlawful enemy combatants" but also to those who are detained awaiting determination whether or not they are unlawful enemy combatants. The vague phrase in the definition of an unlawful enemy combatant that includes anyone "who has purposefully and materially supported hostilities against the United States or its co-belligerent" could be interpreted to include anyone who merely criticizes U.S. policy or the policy of any nation that supports U.S. policy.

61. See *The Boston Globe*, Aug. 6, 2007, p. A1, col. 5.

CHAPTER 4

62. This Proclamation appeared on website www.whitehouse.com, titled "Presidential Christmas Message" and dated December 20, 2001.

63. President's Radio Address, released by the Whitehouse on December 24, 2004, as it appeared on the website www.whitehouse.com. The message states, "At Christmas, we give thanks for the gift of the birth of Christ," and proceeds to interlink Christ, God and the role of U.S. troops in the Middle East.

64. President's Radio Address, released by the Whitehouse on March 26, 2005, as it appeared on the website www.whitehouse.com.

65. See *The Boston Globe*, October 13, 2005, p. A1, col. 1 - 3.

66. See, for example, James A. Morone, *Hellfire Nation: The Politics of Sin in American History,* New Haven and London: Yale Univ. Press, 2003.

67. The corrected version as set forth in Daniel L. Dreisbach, *Thomas Jefferson and the Wall of Separation Between Church and State*, Appendix 6, New York and London: New York Univ. Press, 2002, p. 148.

68. Dreisbach, pp. 63 – 67.

69. Dreisbach, Chapter 4, pp. 55 ff.

70. A. S. Turberville, *Medieval Heresy and the Inquisition*, London: Archon Books, 1964, p. 7.

71. 310 U.S. 296 (1940).

72. See Edward S. Corwin, *The Constitution and What It Means Today*, 13th ed., Princeton, New Jersey: Princeton University Press, 1973, p. 269. The "incorporation" of the Bill of Rights into the Fourteenth Amendment began with *Gitlow v. New York*, 268 U.S. 652 (1925).

73. See, for example, the discussion in Dreisbach, *Thomas Jefferson and the Wall of Separation Between Church and State,* pp. 93, 122 - 23.

74. Frederick Copleston, S.J., *A History of Philosophy,* Vol. 2, Pt. I,

Garden City, NY: Image Books, 1962, p. 104.

75. Turberville, *Medieval Heresy and the Inquisition*, p. 123.

76. Turberville, *Medieval Heresy and the Inquisition*, p. 1.

77. Dreisbach, *Thomas Jefferson and the Wall of Separation Between Church and State*, pp. 76 - 79.

78. Everett Emerson, *John Cotton*, rev. edition, Boston: Twayne Publishers, 1990, pp. 43, 107, 117 - 118; the punishment of heresy was illustrated, for example, by the banishment of Anne Hutchinson, pp. 85 - 94.

79. Frederick Copleston, S.J., *A History of Philosophy*, Vol. 3, Pt. II, Image Books, Garden City, NY, 1963, pp. 70 - 71.

80. Frederick Copleston, S.J., *A History of Philosophy*, Vol. 3, Pt. II, Garden City, NY: Image Books, 1963, p. 91; *Discoveries and Opinions of Galileo*, trans. Stillman Drake. "Epilogue," Garden City, NY: Doubleday Anchor Books, 1957, p. 281.

81. Turberville, *Medieval Heresy and the Inquisition*, p. 1.

82. See note 66 above.

83. Thomas Jefferson, *Notes on the State of Virginia*, originally published 1781 - 1782; quoted in Frank Donovan, *The Thomas Jefferson Papers*, New York: Dodd, Mead & Co., 1963, p. 212.

CHAPTER 5

84. See Gordon M. Fisher, "The Development and History of the U.S. Poverty Thresholds – A Brief Overview," *GSS/SSS Newsletter* [Newsletter of the Government Statistics Section

and the Social Statistics Section of the American Statistical Association], Winter 1977, pp. 6 – 7: http://aspe.os.dhhs.gov/poverty/papers/hptgssiv.htm.

85. "Income, Earnings, and Poverty Data From the 2006 American Community Survey," *U.S. Census Bureau,* August, 2007, p. 26: http://www.census.gov/prod/2007pubs/acs-08.pdf.

86. "Poverty Rate Up 3rd Year In a Row," *Washington Post,* August 27, 2004, p. A01.

87. See, for example, "When Health Insurance is Not a Safeguard," *New York Times,* October 23, 2005.

88. Patient Protection and Affordable Care Act (2010), Section 1501(a)(2)(G) as amended by Section 10106.

89. Report of the American Bankruptcy Institute (abiworld.org), "Consumer Bankruptcy Filings Surge Past One Million During First Nine Months of 2009" (October 2, 2009).

90. See "Minimum Wage Increasingly Lags Poverty Line" by Liana Fox, from the Economic Policy Institute, http://www.epi.org/economic_snapshots/entry/webfeatures_snapshots_20070131/.

91. *Alexander Meiklejohn: Teacher of Freedom*, ed. Cynthia Stokes Brown, Berkeley, CA: Meiklejohn Civil Liberties Institute, 1981, p. 248.

92. *Boston Globe*, March 29, 2005, p. D2, col. 1.

93. The Court's decision is *Citizens United v. Federal Election Commission*, 558 U.S. 50, 130 S.Ct. 876 (2010).

94 . David Talbot, "How Obama Really Did it," *Technology Review,"* Vol. 3, No. 5, Oct. 2008, pp. 78 ff.

95. Pub. L. No. 104-199, 110 Stat. 2419 (Sept. 21, 1996); codified at 1 U.S.C. §7 and 28 U.S.C. §1738C.

96. Summaries of the history of such laws and the arguments for and against them are contained (among other places) in the decision of the Supreme Court of California, *Perez v. Lippold*, 32 Cal.2d 711, 198 P.2d 17 (1948) and the decision of the United States Supreme Court, *Loving v. Virginia*, 388 U.S. 1, 87 S.Ct. 1817 (1967).

97. *Perez v. Lippold*, 32 Cal.2d at 714.

98. *Perez v. Lippold*, 32 Cal.2d at 715.

99. *Loving v. Virginia*, 388 U.S. 1, 87 S.Ct. at 1824 (1967) *(citations omitted)*.

100. 410 U.S. 113; 93 S. Ct. 705 (1973).

101. 410 U.S. at 160; 93 S.Ct. at 730.

102. 410 U.S. at 163; 93 S.Ct. at 731.

103. 410 U.S. at 167; 93 S.Ct. at 733.

104. That "race" is a myth was thoroughly explained many decades ago in Ashley Montagu's *Man's Most Dangerous Myth: The Fallacy of Race*, the first edition of which was published in 1942. (The sixth edition was published in 1998 by AltaMira Press.)

CHAPTER 6

105. See generally Jeffrey Wattles, *The Golden Rule*, New York &

Oxford: Oxford University Press, 1996.

106. See generally Wattles, *The Golden Rule.*

107. The accounting is attributed to Harry Gensler by Wattles, *The Golden Rule*, 137.

108. From a translation of Confucian *Analects*, 15.23, as quoted in Wattles, *The Golden Rule*, 16.

109. From the Dead Sea Scrolls as quoted in Wattles, *The Golden Rule*, 47.

110. Harry J. Gensler, *Formal Ethics*, London: Routledge, 1996, as quoted in Wattles, *The Golden Rule*, 138.

111. Bruce Alton, "An Examination of the Golden Rule," Ph.D. dissertation, Stanford University, 225, as quoted in Wattles, *The Golden Rule*, 135 - 36.

112. Immanuel Kant, *Fundamental Principles of the Metaphysic of Morals*, trans. T. K. Abbott, New York: Liberal Arts Press, 1949, 47 (footnote). Kant's footnote is also discussed in Wattles, *The Golden Rule*, 83 - 86.

113. Kant, *Fundamental Principles*, 47 (footnote).

114. Without going into Kant's philosophy here, we should note that Kant nonetheless thought that the golden guide, though limited, was implied by his own better formulations of moral law. Thus, Kant did not oppose the golden guide generally but thought that it had limitations that his moral maxims did not have. Kant, *Fundamental Principles*, 47 (footnote).

115. Herman Melville, *Moby-Dick*, ed. Harrison Hayford and Herschel Parker, New York: W.W. Norton, 1967, 54, as quoted

in Wattles, *The Golden Rule*, 7.

116. According to Wattles, *The Golden Rule,* 78 - 80 (including notes), they were Bishop William, George Boraston, John Goodman and Benjamin Canfield.

CHAPTER 7

117. Article I, Section 2, #3, apportions representatives by counting free persons as whole persons and "other persons" as three-fifths of a person. This provision was overridden 79 years later by the Fourteenth Amendment, Section 2. However, the same Section 2 of the Fourteenth Amendment explicitly recognized only the voting rights of males.

118. See generally Anthony Lewis, *Freedom for the Thought That We Hate: A Biography of the First Amendment,* New York: Basic Books, 2007.

119. *Whitney v. California,* 274 U.S. 357, 375 (1927) (J. Brandeis, *dissenting*).

INDEX

186

THE AUTHOR

John L. Hodge has sought to understand and advance democratic values in many ways. At Yale University in the 1960's he wrote his Ph.D. dissertation that proposed a philosophical, nonreligious basis for a form of pacifism that allows for self-defense. He was also a draft counselor and peace intern with the American Friends Service Committee in Houston and Seattle. As a college teacher and university professor from 1968-1979, he taught courses addressing racism, sexism, the Vietnam war, and other ethical, social and political issues, mostly at California State University, East Bay. He was a member and chair of the Affirmative Action Committee of a statewide faculty union. After receiving his law degree in 1980, and after serving as Law Clerk for the Massachusetts Appeals Court and Staff Attorney for the U. S. Court of Appeals for the First Circuit, he worked for Massachusetts state agencies that provided health care, such as Medicaid. He directly participated in the successful efforts of these agencies that greatly expanded health care coverage and provided a model for national health care. In addition to this book, he is the main co-author of *Cultural Bases of Racism and Group Oppression: An Examination of Traditional "Western" Concepts, Values and Institutional Structures Which Support Racism, Sexism and Elitism* (1975). He also wrote "Democracy and Free Speech: A Normative Theory of Society and Government," Chapter 5 of *The First Amendment Reconsidered* (1982); and "Equality: Beyond Dualism and Oppression," Chapter 6 of *Anatomy of Racism* (1990). He has an A.B. in mathematics from the University of Kansas (where he graduated as a member of Phi Beta Kappa), a Ph.D. in philosophy from Yale University, and a law degree (J.D.) from the University of California, Berkeley (Boalt Hall). He lives with his wife in the Boston area.